OVERCOMING FEAR

How To Live Peaceful In A Fear-Filled World

CHARLES W MORRIS

Scriptures are taken from the English Standard Version of the Bible

Books may be ordered through booksellers or by contacting:
RSIP
Raising the Standard International Publishing L. L. C.
https://www.rsipublishing.com

RSIP-Charles Morris
https://www.rsiministry.com
Navarre, Florida

ISBN: 9781960641076

Printed in the United States of America
Edition Date: May 2023

Table Of Contents

1
Don't Fear

F ear comes in all shapes and sizes. After all, the world is a scary place right now. However, you don't need to walk in worry, anxiety, and fear. Anxiety and fear flooding our thoughts are some of the biggest causes of unhappiness. Does fear keep you from making certain mental, financial, and relational decisions? Are you stuck in a never-ending thought process of fear? Do you find yourself obsessing and ruminating on things that may or may not happen? Is anxiety, worry, doubt, confusion, depression, and feelings of condemnation consistently attacking your mind and dictating your actions? Here is the plain truth. Fear has countless faces and won't go away on its own.

Sometimes the things that cause us to fear are easily understood by others, such as the fear of snakes and spiders. Other times, the things we may fear might be a joke for others because they don't feel the reality of the anxiety as we do.

Of course, there are extremes, such as the TV show Monk, who seemed afraid of everything. We might understand Monk's fear of heights but then laugh at his fear of milk and germaphobia.

Things like the fear of elevators or crossing a bridge over water might seem foolish to some, yet it is very real to the ones who experience the emotional stronghold of fright when forced to do these things.

What are your fears? How do you deal with and overcome fears that grip you? Fear is not limited to or isolated by a particular social-economical group. Nor are fears different based on educational levels. Even within the Bible, we see many Godly people who faced fears of some kind. Fear is a respecter of none.

If you have lost hope of ever getting free from occasional, persistent, or overwhelming fear and anxiety, take heart! In *"OVERCOMING FEAR,"* I will list the top fourteen fears in the Scriptures that have plagued mankind since their beginning and how the Word tells us we can stand against them. I will show how we can use the Word of God to fight against and overcome the fears that have attacked and defeated us in the past. In this book, you will learn *"How To Live Peaceful In A Fear-Filled World."* If you apply the Scriptures, I fully believe you can exchange your fears for freedom, anxieties for assurance, perplexities for peace, and dread for sweet dreams.

We all experience anxiety. When faced with losing a friend or loved one, what do we do with the fear of death? Even when surrounded by all the conditions for happiness, life can feel incomplete when fear keeps us unfocused and worried about the future. We all have had times when fear surrounds us when there seems to be no way out. At times the fear is so intense it is difficult even to breathe. You know the anxiety I'm speaking about. Your heart is pounding up in your throat and racing wide open like you just ran a hundred-yard dash. Your mind is flooded with dread of everything that might happen, from being hurt, suffocated, robbed, or even killed. The fear could be an MRI machine closing in on you or something that goes "bump" in the middle of the night that startles you out of sleep and may seem silly to others, but it is a very real source of danger to us.

What are we to do when we feel that dread rising up in us and fear starts to cloud our reason? The Word of God says a lot about our emotions and how to bring them captive to our Lord Jesus Christ. Standing before the Father, we are commanded to think and do as His Word teaches. This discipline allows us to start thinking about fear the way the Father thinks about it. Only as we achieve this goal of renewing our minds with God's Word will we possess the power to overcome our fears.

The Word of God confirms God's love for us many times over. It is up to us to believe and receive His love. In 1 John 4:16-19, we see that God is love. The fruit of the Holy Spirit in Galatians 5:22-23 is the very character of the Father. God loves us, and God is love. God gives us joy, and God is joy. God gives us peace, and God is peace.

If asked, "What is the opposite of love?" we would naturally say "hate." Yet the Scriptures do not say there is no hate in love or that love casts out hate. It says in 1 John 4:18 that there is *no fear* in love, and the Father's perfect love *casts out fear*. The same says that fear is punishment or torment. Every place we fear has not been perfected or matured in God's love.

1 John 4:16-19 (ESV) So we have come to know and to believe the love that God has for us. God is love, and whoever abides in love abides in God, and God abides in him. 17 By this is love perfected with us, so that we may have confidence for the day of judgment, because as he is so also are we in this world. 18 There is no fear in love, but perfect love casts out fear. For fear has to do with punishment, and whoever fears has not been perfected in love. 19 We love because he first loved us.

Remember 1 Corinthians 10:13. When the temptation or emotion to fear comes upon us, remember that we have a way of escape so that we can endure the temptation.

> *1 Corinthians 10:13 (ESV) No temptation has overtaken you that is not common to man. God is faithful, and he will not let you be tempted beyond your ability, but with the temptation he will also provide the way of escape, that you may be able to endure it.*

That Which I Am Not To Fear

God the Father delivers us from fear through His Word and His love. If we walk in fear, we have a "Word" problem and a "Love" problem. First, I will list the fourteen fears from God's Word that we can and should be free from then I will go into Scriptural detail on each.

1. *We can be free from the fear of MAN.*
2. *We can be free from the fear of DEATH.*
3. *We can be free from the fear of the FUTURE.*
4. *We can be free from the fear of DANGER.*
5. *We can be free from the fear of IDOLS.*
6. *We can be free from the fear of DREAMS.*
7. *We can be free from the fear of EVIL.*
8. *We can be free from the fear of WAR.*
9. *We can be free from the fear of IMAGINATIONS (Fearful Thinking).*
10. *We can be free from the fear of our ENEMIES.*
11. *We can be free from the fear of PUNISHMENT.*
12. *We can be free from the fear of DARKNESS.*
13. *We can be free from the fear of SPIRITS.*
14. *We can be free from the fear of the SPIRIT OF FEAR.*

Romans 8:14-16 (ESV) For all who are led by the Spirit of God are sons of God. 15 For you did not receive the spirit of slavery to fall back into fear, but you have received the Spirit of adoption as sons, by whom we cry, "Abba! Father!" 16 The Spirit himself bears witness with our spirit that we are children of God,

2
Overcoming the Fear of MAN

1. We Can Be Free From The Fear Of MAN.

As long as we walk in fear of man, we will be people pleasers. We will try to make ourselves accepted in the eyes of man instead of the eyes of God. Have you ever gone "along" with someone, a group, or a large crowd knowing deep inside it was not really what you felt, believed, or would have done? Did you ever cave into peer pressure because you did not want to be the "third man out?" We all desire to be liked and to belong in a group. No one expects to stand among people and feel alone. I get this. However, if we do not guard our hearts, we will allow this loneliness and the strong desire to "fit in" to cause us to be people pleasers. If we are people-pleasers, we will walk in the fear of being rejected. This is how the fear of man is manifested.

This type of giving in to please others is dangerous, and for pastors, this is extremely dangerous because the pastor will become a hireling instead of a shepherd. This fear of man will also keep us from making deep covenant relationships. When we are people pleasers, we will follow the old saying, "If you can't be with the one you love, then love the one you're with." We will be double-minded and unstable in all our ways if we walk in fear of man. When we fear someone, we are allowing that person to control us. Our fear gives them the keys to our thoughts, emotions, and actions. In other words, they drive our bus.

So, what do we do? How do we stop being a man-pleaser because the bottom line is that we have a fear of men, meaning we have a fear of being rejected and left out? To overcome this, we must see what the Bible declares is the opposite of fear and learn to walk in it. The Bible tells us to renew our minds with His Word.

God is our shield and reward.

God is our shield, fortress, and protector. God told Abram to "fear not." Then He relayed to Abram why he was not to fear.

> *Genesis 15:1 (ESV) After these things the word of the LORD came to Abram in a vision: "Fear not, Abram, I am your shield; your reward shall be very great."*

Fear God over man.

Our Lord Jesus Christ told us not to fear man even if it meant physical death. However, we are to fear God, who has the authority to cast people into hell.

> *Luke 12:4-5 (ESV) "I tell you, my friends, do not fear those who kill the body, and after that have nothing more that they can do. 5 But I will warn you whom to fear: fear him who, after he has killed, has authority to cast into hell. Yes, I tell you, fear him!*

What can man do?

The writer of Hebrews restated what our Lord said in Luke 12:4. The Lord is my helper, so what can man do to me? If he kills me, I will spend eternity in glory with my

Lord. If men beat me for righteousness' sake, my Father will bless me. Fear of man can be overcome when we see that we have a win-win situation as believers walking in truth and faith.

> Hebrews 13:6 (ESV) So we can confidently say, "The Lord is my helper; I will not fear; what can man do to me?"

The Father will not forsake us.

Psalms 37:23-25 gives us a great promise of welfare as our Father watches over us.

> Psalms 37:23-25 (ESV) The steps of a man are established by the LORD, when he delights in his way; 24 though he fall, he shall not be cast headlong, for the LORD upholds his hand. 25 I have been young, and now am old, yet I have not seen the righteous forsaken or his children begging for bread.

Whom shall I fear?

We need to embrace the mindset and heart of David when he made these statements in Psalms 27:1-3. "Whom shall I fear?" "Whom shall I be afraid?" "My heart shall not fear."

> Psalms 27:1-3 (ESV) Of David. The LORD is my light and my salvation; whom shall I fear? The LORD is the stronghold of my life; of whom shall I be afraid? 2 When evildoers assail me to eat up my flesh, my adversaries and foes, it is they who stumble and fall. 3 Though an army encamp against me, my heart shall

not fear; though war arise against me, yet I will be confident.

Take refuge in the Lord.

Psalms 118:6-12 gives us a clear answer for anyone who walks in fear of man. It is taking refuge in the Lord.

Psalms 118:6-12 (ESV) The LORD is on my side; I will not fear. What can man do to me? 7 The LORD is on my side as my helper; I shall look in triumph on those who hate me. 8 It is better to take refuge in the LORD than to trust in man. 9 It is better to take refuge in the LORD than to trust in princes. 10 All nations surrounded me; in the name of the LORD I cut them off! 11 They surrounded me, surrounded me on every side; in the name of the LORD I cut them off! 12 They surrounded me like bees; they went out like a fire among thorns; in the name of the LORD I cut them off!

I don't want to sound simplistic, but our victory over the fear of man is not some complicated formula. According to the many Scriptures, we just read, it comes down to trusting God and His Word daily. It is choosing each day by faith that if God be for us, who can be against us? The Father is our shield, fortress, refuge, and protector. As long as I maintain my life under His grace by faith, then His hand of protection covers me. Will trials and tribulations come? Yes! But these serve a greater purpose of moving me from faith to faith and grace to grace. Gold is purified by fire. Love and fear God; you will find that pleasing Him has far more significant benefits than trying to be a man-pleaser.

3
Overcoming the Fear of DEATH

1. We can be free from the fear of MAN.
2. We can be free from the fear of DEATH.

Unless the Lord returns, we will all die sometime in the future! Have you had loved ones or friends pass away? Have you had near-death experiences? Have you had something traumatic happen in your life that opened the door to an unhealthy fear of death?

Let's start by establishing some Biblical facts, and then I will share some personal experiences with death. Death is not a loss unless we are spiritually lost. I hear believers talking about a loved one who has died, and they say, "I lost my dad or mom, etc." As believers, we are not lost in death, only separated for a period of time. Those spiritually lost will spend eternity in hell, and those who are saved will spend eternity with God the Father, first in heaven, then on the new earth and new city. Everyone will live forever. I know that the heart pain of losing a loved one or friend can hurt for many years and leave a vacuum that seems as big as consuming as "a black hole."

Let me share some of my death and near-death experiences. My first memory of death was when my older cousin and his wife died in a car wreck when I was about five years old. I didn't understand much about what was happening except seeing my parents, grandparents, and all of my aunts and uncles gathered together and weeping at my grandparents' house. I remember feeling sad and fearful about the bits and pieces of information I gleaned from the conversations around the living room and out in the yard. I remember seeing the sadness on the faces of my family members and hearing the fear in their voices. During those first hours when everyone came together to grieve, I kept hearing the statement, "This could happen to any of us."

One year later, when I was only six, my grandfather died suddenly of a heart attack. He and I were very close, and this affected me greatly. Then over a short period, I had uncles, aunts, cousins, and nieces die suddenly from sicknesses, car accidents, or drug overdoses. The realization of death had made a significant impact on me.

Moving ahead many years, I was married, saved, and called into the pastoral ministry. Suddenly, without any warning at age 25, I found myself in a hospital facing open heart surgery for a massive hole in my heart. The doctor said I had a 50/50 chance of making it through the surgery and only a 20% chance I would ever be able to work again. They proclaimed that because of the intense damage to the heart, I would be a cardiac cripple. This diagnosis was a major blow emotionally and mentally. I would not have gotten through it except for God's Word renewing my mind that He had a plan and a purpose for me, and I would be declared a miracle boy.

During the surgery, the doctors said the machine they had my body on pumping blood got a bubble in it that went to my brain. The heart operation was successful, but they kept me in an induced coma for three days. They told my wife they didn't know what to expect when I came out of the coma because it depended on where the bubble was lodged. I could go into a coma, be blind, be deaf, be paralyzed, or be mute. It was all based on the brain's damage caused by this bubble. The heart surgery had been on a Wednesday morning. I woke up on a Friday night, although I had no idea what day it was. I began to unplug all the cables and pull out the wires I was attached to or was attached to me. I got out of bed, walked out of the room, and went to the TV room. The nurses at their station saw that my monitor reading flatlined and ran to the room, expecting that my heart had stopped. I could only imagine the expression on their face when they found that I wasn't dead. Bless God; I was just absent. So, they quickly started searching for me and found me in the TV room. They took me back to my room, scolded me, and told me not to leave my bed. The following day the doctor walked into the room, and the first words out of his mouth were, "How is my miracle boy?"

It was this experience of my open-heart surgery that God set me free from the fear of death. I realized what the Apostle Paul had said concerning death. To be absent from the body is to be present with the Lord. Many people are like Hezekiah in 2 Kings chapter 20. He was sick unto death and cried out to the Lord for fifteen more years. Everybody wants to go to heaven, but nobody wants to die. I'm not ready to catch the next bus to heaven because, like Hezekiah, I still believe the Father has much for me to do. I will say this lightly because I'm actively involved in the Kingdom ministry.

I'm not a couch potato just sitting watching TV, talking about what God might use me for. I'm not sadistic with a death wish, but I do not fear death. I have asked my family to have a celebration time of a life well lived when it comes my time to pass from this side of eternity to the next side. There is such freedom when we overcome the fear of man and the fear of death. All other fears are actually under the umbrella of these two. If we no longer fear what man can do to us or what death can do to us, all other fears seem

12

insignificant. Overcoming the fear of death and the fear of man is not a one-and-done situation. We all want to see friends and relatives grow up. We want to see our children grow up and get married. We want to see our grandkids and great-grandkids and witness what they will become. But either the Bible is true, or it's not. In reality, it seems a little foolish that we would spend so much time trying to protect this mortal body for 70 or 80 years when we have an endless eternity to spend in glory with the Father.

When a loved one who is saved dies, that means they got to heaven before the throne of God before you did. They are not lost from you. When people who are not saved die, they will be forever separated from God and you.

We should grow to embrace the attitude of Paul and look forward to death and being with our Lord Jesus Christ. Death is not a period but just a comma. Death for a believer means that we passed from this life to the next life because only the body died.

God's Word records the death of loved ones.

The death of loved ones is familiar to us as it was to the Saints in the Bible. In Genesis 35:12-19 we see that Jacob's beloved wife, Rachel died in childbirth.

> *Genesis 35:12-19 (ESV) The land that I gave to Abraham and Isaac I will give to you, and I will give the land to your offspring after you." 13 Then God went up from him in the place where he had spoken with him. 14 And Jacob set up a pillar in the place where he had spoken with him, a pillar of stone. He poured out a drink offering on it and poured oil on it. 15 So Jacob called the name of the place where God had spoken with him Bethel. 16 Then they journeyed*

from Bethel. When they were still some distance from Ephrath, Rachel went into labor, and she had hard labor. 17 And when her labor was at its hardest, the midwife said to her, "Do not fear, for you have another son." 18 And as her soul was departing (for she was dying), she called his name Ben-oni; but his father called him Benjamin. 19 So Rachel died, and she was buried on the way to Ephrath (that is, Bethlehem),

There were three strongholds the enemy had power over. He controlled sin, death, and the grave. We see in Hebrews 2:14-15 that when our Lord Jesus Christ died on the cross for mankind, He defeated the enemy's stronghold of sin over us. When He rose from the dead, Jesus defeated the strongholds that death and the grave had over us.

Sin, Death, and the Grave have been defeated.

Hebrews 2:14-15 (ESV) Since therefore the children share in flesh and blood, he himself likewise partook of the same things, that through death he might destroy the one who has the power of death, that is, the devil, 15 and deliver all those who through fear of death were subject to lifelong slavery.

We start the dying process at birth.

Yes, our corruptible bodies of flesh and bones are dying. We either get old or get gone. At birth, we start aging because our days are numbered, and our outer man is perishing.

2 Corinthians 4:16-18 (ESV) So we do not lose heart. Though our outer self is wasting away, our inner self is being renewed day by day. 17 For this light momentary affliction is preparing for us an eternal weight of glory beyond all comparison, 18 as we look not to the things that are seen but to the things that are unseen. For the things that are seen are transient, but the things that are unseen are eternal.

Our outer man may be perishing, but praise be to God that in the twinkling of an eye and the blast of the trumpet, we will be changed and raised to new glorified bodies. We see in 1 Corinthians 15:52-57 that for the believer, death is but for a moment, but life is everlasting.

Believers will put on new glorified bodies.

1 Corinthians 15:52-57 (ESV) in a moment, in the twinkling of an eye, at the last trumpet. For the trumpet will sound, and the dead will be raised imperishable, and we shall be changed. 53 For this perishable body must put on the imperishable, and this mortal body must put on immortality. 54 When the perishable puts on the imperishable, and the mortal puts on immortality, then shall come to pass the saying that is written: "Death is swallowed up in victory." 55 "O death, where is your victory? O death, where is your sting?" 56 The sting of death is sin, and the power of sin is the law. 57 But thanks be to God, who gives us the victory through our Lord Jesus Christ.

Again, remember that Jesus has defeated death and the grave.

If we believe the Word of God, we know that death has been defeated, and we will move from this life to live before the Father in His kingdom. Oh, what a glorious day.

15

Isaiah 25:8 (ESV) He will swallow up death forever; and the Lord GOD will wipe away tears from all faces, and the reproach of his people he will take away from all the earth, for the LORD has spoken.

Job knew about the resurrection from death.

We tend to speak a lot about Job's patience and righteousness. However, in Job 19:25-26 we see his prophetic insight. Job knew that one day he would die. But he also knew that even after his fleshly body was decayed, he would see God in his new glorified body. What an incredible revelation.

Job 19:25-26 (ESV) For I know that my Redeemer lives, and at the last he will stand upon the earth. 26 And after my skin has been thus destroyed, yet in my flesh I shall see God,

Father, be honored in me, in my life and my death.

The Bible encourages and warns us to start right, run right, and finish right. We should embrace Paul's statement in Philippians 1:20-24 that the Father would be glorified and honored in our life and death. We should always find ourselves struggling between desiring to die and be with Christ and living to share Christ with others. We should not find ourselves just trying to hold on, protect, and squeeze every second of life because we are afraid to die.

Philippians 1:20-24 (ESV) as it is my eager expectation and hope that I will not be at all ashamed, but that with full courage now as always Christ will be honored in my body, whether by life or by death. 21 For to me to live is Christ, and to die is gain. 22 If I am to live in the flesh, that means fruitful labor for me. Yet which I shall choose I cannot tell. 23 I am hard pressed between the two. My desire is to depart and be with Christ, for that is far better. 24 But to remain in the flesh is more necessary on your account.

Death will not separate the believer from God and His love.

Death will separate us from religion and the things that we associate with our walk with God, such as a church or our Bibles. Death will separate us for a while from our Christian friends and Christian family members. However, death cannot separate us from God's love. In death, we will see Him as He is, in all His glory and love.

Romans 8:35-39 (ESV) Who shall separate us from the love of Christ? Shall tribulation, or distress, or persecution, or famine, or nakedness, or danger, or sword? 36 As it is written, "For your sake we are being killed all the day long; we are regarded as sheep to be slaughtered." 37 No, in all these things we are more than conquerors through him who loved us. 38 For I am sure that neither death nor life, nor angels nor rulers, nor things present nor things to come, nor powers, 39 nor height nor depth, nor anything else in all creation, will be able to separate us from the love of God in Christ Jesus our Lord.

4

Overcoming Fear of the FUTURE

1. *We can be free from the fear of MAN.*
2. *We can be free from the fear of DEATH.*
3. *We can be free from the fear of the FUTURE.*

There is a Christian song from years ago with a line that says, "I don't know what the future holds, but I know who holds the future." What a great truth. However, let's take about the daily down-and-dirty fact. Lawlessness has filled our land. Unemployment is at an all-time high. Gas and food prices are skyrocketing as inflation has all but completely crippled our country. Many in our Country want more money without working. Businesses are being forced to shut down because they cannot find people willing to put in a day's work. Crime, especially violent crime, is totally out of control while our Police force is belittled, ridiculed, undermined, and deemed hand-cuffed from enforcing law and order. Sexual immorality has passed any form of science or logic. Evil is called good, while good is called evil.

So, what are we to do when facing unemployment because our company goes under? How can we protect our children when sex offenders are heralded as champions of progressive thought? How do we cope in a society where men and women defy logic and science and are not even intelligent enough to know their birth gender? How do we handle the thoughts and fears of the possibility of being shot down in a mall, store, on the street, or in our cars by random acts of uncontrolled violence? How do we face the fear that we cannot protect our children in their schools as we witness kids killing kids? We have every opportunity to fear in our days, and the Bible says things will get worse. How do we overcome the fear of the future?

The acronym for F.E.A.R. is **False Evidence Appearing Real**. I hear a lot of conversations from believers that can only be classified as fear as they converse about the gloom and doom of what "might be." Our walk with God is not dictated by our President, the status of the economy, our health, the prevailing lawlessness of an amoral society, or the job situation. God, the Father, knows what we need and when we need it. He has a destiny for us and is more committed to it than we are.

Do not fear; just do what God says.

In Genesis 46:1-3 we see that Jacob had no idea what God was up to and where He was leading him, but Jacob knew he had a destiny to fulfill. God told him not to fear.

> *Genesis 46:1-3 (ESV) So Israel took his journey with all that he had and came to Beersheba, and offered sacrifices to the God of his father Isaac. 2 And God spoke to Israel in visions of the night and said, "Jacob, Jacob." And he said, "Here I am." 3 Then he said, "I am God, the God of your father. Do not be afraid to go down to Egypt, for there I will make you into a great nation.*

When men intend evil for us, remember God has a different plan.

In Genesis 50:19-20 Joseph told his brothers not to fear. He comforted them with the message that they intended evil in their actions, but God had a plan that was good for Joseph and many nations.

> *Genesis 50:19-20 (ESV) But Joseph said to them, "Do not fear, for am I in the place of God? 20 As for you, you meant evil against me, but God meant it for good, to bring it about that many people should be kept alive, as they are today.*

Jesus commanded us not to worry or fear.

The Father has called us to more than breathe air and sit on our blessed assurance as believers. He wants us to be people of His Word and people of faith. The Father said He would guide the steps of a righteous man, and His Word in us will accomplish in and through us what God intended. He told us not to worry or fear about tomorrow or what we will wear or eat.

> *Matthew 6:25-32 (ESV) "Therefore I tell you, do not be anxious about your life, what you will eat or what you will drink, nor about your body, what you will put on. Is not life more than food, and the body more than clothing? 26 Look at the birds of the air: they neither sow nor reap nor gather into barns, and yet your heavenly Father feeds them. Are you not of more value than they? 27 And which of you by being anxious can add a single hour to his span of life? 28 And why are you anxious about clothing? Consider the lilies of the field, how they grow: they neither toil nor spin, 29 yet I tell you, even Solomon in all his glory was not arrayed like one of these. 30 But if God so clothes the grass of the field, which today is alive and tomorrow is thrown into the oven, will he not much more clothe you, O you of little faith? 31*

Therefore do not be anxious, saying, 'What shall we eat?' or 'What shall we drink?' or 'What shall we wear?' 32 For the Gentiles seek after all these things, and your heavenly Father knows that you need them all.

The bottom line is this. The world is going to get worse. People will become more angry, deceitful, violent, and immoral. Christians and Jews are going to be hated beyond what we imagined. Jesus said, "If they hate me, how much more will they hate you." I know this is one of the "much more" statements from the Bible that none of us is looking forward to.

According to Matthew 24 and parallel Scriptures, the future looks bleak if we view it from the position of our flesh. However, we lose any fear of the future if we focus on the truth of God's Word and walk in the Spirit and faith. What the flesh sees as the point of no return, our spirit views as joy unspeakable and full of glory. We will fear if we walk under our circumstances. We will walk boldly as lions when we walk positioned above our circumstances.

5
Overcoming the Fear of DANGER

1. *We can be free from the fear of MAN.*
2. *We can be free from the fear of DEATH.*
3. *We can be free from the fear of the FUTURE.*
4. *We can be free from the fear of DANGER.*

Fear of danger or the unknown can paralyze us to the point that we do nothing. What risk do you fear that paralyzes you in attempting other activities? Did you have a traumatic event that has caused a stronghold of the fear of danger to be built in your heart?

When I was a young boy, I almost drowned twice. These events instilled a deadly fear in me that caused me to view all creeks, rivers, ponds, or oceans as danger hazards that should be avoided at all costs. As a result, I grew into adulthood without the ability to swim or enjoy any water sports. It was years before I learned to swim and face my fears of entering lakes, rivers, and oceans.

Dangers are lurking around every corner. Sometimes I wonder how my generation survived childhood. We rode bikes without helmets and many times without brakes. Our parent's cars did not have seat belts, and no one used them if they were installed. We rode down the freeways bouncing around in the back of our friend's pickup trucks.

Many believers are fearful of taking a risk. This fear is one of the reasons why so many believers hesitate to share their testimony of faith. For some reason, they fear there is danger tied to sharing our testimony.

A day is coming when sharing your testimony could be a life and death situation, but that day is not among us yet in America or Europe. I would rather aim at something and miss it than aim at nothing and hit it every time. What are we willing to do today BY FAITH that if God does not come through, we will look like fools? Walking with the Lord Jesus Christ is a risk-taking profession.

Take a risk. Don't die in Egypt.

The people of Israel would have rather died as enslaved people in Egypt than risk everything and see the hand of God move in a mighty way.

> *Exodus 14:10-14 (ESV) When Pharaoh drew near, the people of Israel lifted up their eyes, and behold, the Egyptians were marching after them, and they feared greatly. And the people of Israel cried out to the LORD. 11 They said to Moses, "Is it because there are no graves in Egypt that you have taken us away to die in the wilderness? What have you done to us in bringing us out of Egypt? 12 Is not this what we said to you in Egypt: 'Leave us alone that we may serve the Egyptians'? For it would have been better for us to serve the Egyptians than to die in the wilderness." 13 And Moses said to the people, "Fear not, stand firm, and see the salvation of the LORD, which he will work for you today. For the Egyptians whom you see today, you shall never see again. 14 The LORD will fight for you, and you have only to be silent."*

All businessmen have to take risks and face the danger of failure. No risk, no reward. This risk-taking goes deeper than just business. When we don't take risks, we miss out on what God is doing. We miss out on seeing God work. We miss out on a testimony. We miss out on a blessing. If you think about it, it is riskier not to take risks. Don't let the fear of danger keep you from stepping out of the boat in faith.

Trust God and don't fear the danger. Why? Because there are strange things afoot.

King Solomon coined these words in Ecclesiastes 11:4-6, by direction of the inspiration of the Holy Spirit. He is saying to take a risk. Don't just stare at the clouds. Face the danger and sow something in your life. Just like we don't understand how God forms the child in the womb, we won't know the complete plans of God in our lives. This includes difficult times.

> *Ecclesiastes 11:4-6 (ESV) He who observes the wind will not sow, and he who regards the clouds will not reap. 5 As you do not know the way the spirit comes to the bones in the womb of a woman with child, so you do not know the work of God who makes everything. 6 In the morning sow your seed, and at evening withhold not your hand, for you do not know which will prosper, this or that, or whether both alike will be good.*

In Ecclesiastes 10:7-9, King Solomon states that he has seen a lot of strange things. Solomon is telling us that there is danger in everything. He saw enslaved people riding while princes were on foot. A man must dig a hole for his job, only to fall into it. A man tears down a wall only to get bit by a snake. A man digging stones out of a quarry to build homes is hurt by the rocks. Men who split logs to build a house and furniture are always in danger from the activity. King

Solomon instructs us that life is a risk, and we must face the threats and live it out.

> *Ecclesiastes 10:7-9 (ESV) I have seen slaves on horses, and princes walking on the ground like slaves. 8 He who digs a pit will fall into it, and a serpent will bite him who breaks through a wall. 9 He who quarries stones is hurt by them, and he who splits logs is endangered by them.*

Disobedience to God is the real danger.

Disregarding God's voice when He tells us to do something is dangerous. Sometimes the risk that God tells us to take is protecting us from something far more dangerous in the future. Sometimes the risk is going to be beneficial to others. Always remember, our heavenly Father always knows best. In 1 Chronicles 28:20, King David instructed his son, Solomon, to be strong and courageous. He told him not to be afraid no matter what he faced. God would not let David build the Temple because he was a man of war and had shed too much blood. It was going to be a mighty task given to his son Solomon.

> *1 Chronicles 28:20 (ESV) Then David said to Solomon his son, "Be strong and courageous and do it. Do not be afraid and do not be dismayed, for the LORD God, even my God, is with you. He will not leave you or forsake you, until all the work for the service of the house of the LORD is finished.*

Why do we call see danger in certain things and not in others?

When we face a situation and deem it dangerous, we must ask ourselves, "Why is it a risk." Do we consider it hazardous because we judge it by our weaknesses and inexperience? Do we believe something is dangerous because of our bad experience or lack of experience? Let's look at why Gideon felt his situation was deemed dangerous and then view what God told him about it.

When God called Gideon a mighty man, Gideon looked at his upbringing and could only see his failures and shortcomings. Therefore, he feared what was coming. However, God reminded Gideon that He would be with him.

> *Judges 6:12 (ESV) And the angel of the LORD appeared to him and said to him, "The LORD is with you, O mighty man of valor."*

> *Judges 6:14-16 (ESV) And the LORD turned to him and said, "Go in this might of yours and save Israel from the hand of Midian; do not I send you?" 15 And he said to him, "Please, Lord, how can I save Israel? Behold, my clan is the weakest in Manasseh, and I am the least in my father's house." 16 And the LORD said to him, "But I will be with you, and you shall strike the Midianites as one man."*

Being fearful of possible or probable danger does not change the situation.

Worrying and being afraid don't change a thing. It stops us from getting what we desire as children in our walk with our Lord Jesus Christ. One of the most painful things in this world is living with regret. You don't want to say to yourself, "I wish I would have taken a chance." We settle for nothing when we don't face danger and take risks. We have the opportunity to change our entire future if we overcome our fear of danger.

Remember the parable of the talents. The man who was given one talent was afraid to take the risk of losing it. To him, the danger of losing the one talent was greater than the risk of gaining two. The consequences of acting in fear of danger cost him more than he wanted to pay.

Matthew 25:14-18 (ESV) "For it will be like a man going on a journey, who called his servants and entrusted to them his property. 15 To one he gave five talents, to another two, to another one, to each according to his ability. Then he went away. 16 He who had received the five talents went at once and traded with them, and he made five talents more. 17 So also he who had the two talents made two talents more. 18 But he who had received the one talent went and dug in the ground and hid his master's money.

What was the result of those who took risks with the talents they received?

Matthew 25:20-23 (ESV) And he who had received the five talents came forward, bringing five talents more, saying, 'Master, you delivered to me five talents; here, I have made five talents more.' 21 His master said to him, 'Well done, good and faithful servant. You have been faithful over a little; I will set you over much. Enter into the joy of your master.' 22 And he also who had the two talents came forward, saying, 'Master, you delivered to me two talents; here, I have made two talents more.' 23 His master said to him, 'Well done, good and faithful servant. You have been faithful over a little; I will set you over much. Enter into the joy of your master.'

What was the result of the man who "played it safe" with the one talent he had received?

Matthew 25:24-30 (ESV) He also who had received the one talent came forward, saying, 'Master, I knew you to be a hard man, reaping where you did not sow, and gathering where you scattered no seed, 25 so I was afraid, and I went and hid your talent in the ground. Here, you have what is yours.' 26 But his master answered him, 'You wicked and slothful servant! You knew that I reap where I have not sown and gather where I scattered no seed? 27 Then you ought to have invested my money with the bankers, and at my coming I should have received what was my own with interest. 28 So take the talent from him and give it to him who has the ten talents. 29 For to everyone who has will more be given, and he will have an abundance. But from the one who has not, even what he has will be taken away. 30 And cast the worthless servant into the outer darkness. In that place there will be weeping and gnashing of teeth.'

A popular quote says, "If God brings you to it, He will bring you through it." We always think we have strong faith until a situation arises, and we must exercise that faith.

6
Overcoming the Fear of IDOLS

1. *We can be free from the fear of MAN.*
2. *We can be free from the fear of DEATH.*
3. *We can be free from the fear of the FUTURE.*
4. *We can be free from the fear of DANGER.*
5. *We can be free from the fear of IDOLS.*

Idols are man-made and have no power. We should not fear them. We are to fear only one true God: the Lord God of Abraham, Isaac, and Jacob. The problem is that we may not recognize or be truthful about having an idol. I guess the first thing to do is to give the term "idol" a Biblical definition. Any person or thing that consumes your thoughts, words, time, energy, or money other than God is an idol. The Scriptures are clear about having an idol established in our hearts.

Exodus 20:4 (ESV) "You shall not make for yourself a carved image, or any likeness of anything that is in heaven above, or that is in the earth beneath, or that is in the water under the earth.

Deuteronomy 5:8 (ESV) "'You shall not make for yourself a carved image, or any likeness of anything that is in heaven above, or that is on the earth beneath, or that is in the water under the earth.

The commandment raises the issue of idolatry. Idols are gods of our creation, gods that we feel will give us what we want or need in our thoughts, emotions, physical, or resources. In the Old Testament, we saw that an idol was an image or anything used as an object of worship in place of God. An idol can be a religious image or a person who we admire and maybe even seem to worship. We seldom would think that a cherished and respected person or thing can become an idol.

Think about the things that could be idols we have knowingly or unconsciously established in our hearts. It could be our health, job hobbies, or finances. Let's bring it closer to home. An idol could be our spouse, children, or grandchildren. I have heard Christian men ignorantly say they idolized their spouses. Yes, we are to love our spouse, children, and grandchildren. However, they are not to take the place emotionally, mentally, or in any other capacity over our time and worship of God.

Under the inspiration of the Holy Spirit, Paul stated that whatever does not proceed from faith is a sin.

> Romans 14:23 (ESV) But whoever has doubts is condemned if he eats, because the eating is not from faith. For whatever does not proceed from faith is sin.

The Old Testament commands us not to fear idols.

The inhabitants of every section of land the Israelites were called to go in and possess worshipped different idols. God told them not to fear these false gods.

> Judges 6:9-10 (ESV) And I delivered you from the hand of the Egyptians and from the hand of all who oppressed you, and drove them out before you and gave you their land. 10 And I said to you, 'I am the LORD your God; you shall not fear the gods of the

Amorites in whose land you dwell.' But you have not obeyed my voice."

God's people were always commanded not to fear the gods and idols that others worshipped and sacrificed to. We need to hear this message because it would seem that America has bowed a knee to false gods because of fear of reprisal of terrorism from those who worship these false gods. Three times in 2 Kings 17:35-39, the statement "You shall not fear other gods" is used. This fear is real, and everyone in all nations will face the opportunity to either fear the false gods or to bow to the one true God.

2 Kings 17:35-39 (ESV) The LORD made a covenant with them and commanded them, "You shall not fear other gods or bow yourselves to them or serve them or sacrifice to them, 36 but you shall fear the LORD, who brought you out of the land of Egypt with great power and with an outstretched arm. You shall bow yourselves to him, and to him you shall sacrifice. 37 And the statutes and the rules and the law and the commandment that he wrote for you, you shall always be careful to do. You shall not fear other gods, 38 and you shall not forget the covenant that I have made with you. You shall not fear other gods, 39 but you shall fear the LORD your God, and he will deliver you out of the hand of all your enemies."

How should we think and act toward idols?

Paul tells us how to think and act toward the idols and false gods established among us. In a nonchalant way, Paul says, "Hey, don't waste time on them; they don't exist." There is only one God that exists and is all-powerful.

Everything owes its existence to the Lord God of heaven and earth.

> *1 Corinthians 8:3-6 (ESV) But if anyone loves God, he is known by God. 4 Therefore, as to the eating of food offered to idols, we know that "an idol has no real existence," and that "there is no God but one." 5 For although there may be so-called gods in heaven or on earth—as indeed there are many "gods" and many "lords"— 6 yet for us there is one God, the Father, from whom are all things and for whom we exist, and one Lord, Jesus Christ, through whom are all things and through whom we exist.*

How do we overcome the fear of idols?

   1. REST IN GOD'S CREATIVE PLAN.

Nothing on this earth was designed to satisfy our fleshly desires. Our satisfaction should come from God only.

   2. MEDITATE AND FOCUS ON THE CREATOR.

We are to give a quick glance at what the world offers, but our steady gaze should be on the Father. Since our heavenly Father determines the creative plan and design of all good things, trust Him for your daily needs. The best things in this world are a shadow of God's goodness and resources.

   3. REMEMBER THAT WE ARE PERISHING DAILY.

One of the ways we protect ourselves from good things becoming idols is by remembering that our days are numbered. Death is the equalizer of all mankind. The fact that we all will one day die and can't take our treasures with us puts everything in the proper perspective.

Solomon emphasizes in the book of Ecclesiastes that mankind is fragile and temporary. We must recognize the vanity of trying to hold on to things we so quickly idolize. We must measure and judge them for what they are. The things of this world are earthly and unable to supply our deepest needs and desires. Only our heavenly Father can satisfy the longings of our hearts.

Job loved his family, servants, cattle, and his health. In a short time, the enemy took all of these from him. We have all read that Job was a righteous man and loved God. However, what was in Job's heart that needed to be touched by the Father? It was his fear of losing everything. Everything he had, including his family, had become an idol in his heart. Look at what Job said when he lost everything.

Job 3:25 (ESV) For the thing that I fear comes upon me, and what I dread befalls me.

Job had a great fear of losing his family, servants, possessions, and health. Why? Because each of these things had an unhealthy position in his heart.

4. BE CONTENT IN ALL CIRCUMSTANCES.

Perhaps the most difficult and yet most secure step to implement to overcome the fear of idols is simply practicing the position of contentment.

Philippians 4:11-13 (ESV) Not that I am speaking of being in need, for I have learned in whatever situation I am to be content. 12 I know how to be brought low, and I know how to abound. In any and every circumstance, I have learned the secret of facing plenty and hunger, abundance and need. 13 I can do all things through him who strengthens me.

7
Overcoming the Fear of DREAMS

1. *We can be free from the fear of MAN.*
2. *We can be free from the fear of DEATH.*
3. *We can be free from the fear of the FUTURE.*
4. *We can be free from the fear of DANGER.*
5. *We can be free from the fear of IDOLS.*
6. *We can be free from the fear of DREAMS.*

Dreams and nightmares should not bring about fear, but sometimes they do. The enemy can work overtime on our imagination, disrupting sleep and rest time. Have you had nights where you dreamed harmful or sinful dreams? Have you had recurring nightmares? Is your body exhausted, but your mind runs wild at night when you hope to grab some shuteye?

Dreams are a routine activity of the sleeping process. We typically dream in many small segments totaling about an hour a night. Many people say they don't dream, but they do. The issue is they don't remember their dreams. Dreaming is not the problem. The point is when we fear our dreams because they disturb us for some reason. A loved one or we might get hurt or hunted in our dreams, causing us a sense of fleeing something or someone seeking harm. One of the common disturbing dreams is a sense of falling or drowning. Another typical dream that is disturbing involves sexual or lust-filled dreams. I have spoken to many who suffered these types of recurring dreams or nightmares.

Dreams from God.

Dreams and nightmares are nothing more than imaginations at work while we sleep. Before someone gets upset over this statement, I am speaking about dreams from the enemy and our conscience. I am not talking about dreams given by God for any number of various reasons. Dreams given by God the Father can be disturbing as they can reveal life-and-death situations.

A lady in our church in Germany had a dream that I was driving a truck back in the States and that a car hit me, and I wrecked and died in the crash. I could have dismissed the dream for a lot of reasons. Number one, I did not own a truck, and I had no plans on buying or renting one, and I have only driven one a few times in my entire life. The second reason I could have dismissed this dream was that I lived in Germany and had no plans to return to the States immediately. But, in the Spirit, I believed this dream was from God and was a message, a warning for me of something that could happen. So, we had a prayer time and believed that God the Father had sealed me in His protection.

A few days later, a Christian brother contacted me, who said he was moving his household goods from Alabama to Germany to live. If I had any household items left in Florida that I wanted him to ship to Germany, I needed to get them to him. In no time, I found myself back in the States driving a truck full of furniture from Florida to Alabama on the Interstate. A car passed me and then lost control. He flipped in front of me, missing the truck by mere inches. I stopped and helped the man driving the car until the police arrived. I know my life was spared because of God's warning to that lady in the church, her obedience in sharing, and our prayer of faith.

Joel 2:28 (ESV) "And it shall come to pass afterward, that I will pour out my Spirit on all flesh; your sons and your daughters shall prophesy, your old men shall dream dreams, and your young men shall see visions. Acts 2:16-17 (ESV) But this is what was uttered through the prophet Joel: 17 "'And in the last days it shall be, God declares, that I will pour out my Spirit on all flesh, and your sons and your daughters shall prophesy, and your young men shall see visions, and your old men shall dream dreams;

Job had disturbing and alarming dreams from God. In the Old and New Testaments, most who followed God had dreams from heaven that were warnings, instructions, directions, or messages of encouragement.

Fearful dreams from God as warnings.

Job 4:12-15 (ESV) "Now a word was brought to me stealthily; my ear received the whisper of it. 13 Amid thoughts from visions of the night, when deep sleep falls on men, 14 dread came upon me, and trembling, which made all my bones shake. 15 A spirit glided past my face; the hair of my flesh stood up.

I became a Christ on September 4th, 1974, when I surrendered my life to the Lord Jesus Christ. I sought to walk in the Spirit and holiness in every area of my life. However, my dreams betrayed me. In my dreams, the enemy seemed to have me defeated through very ungodly perverted dreams. It was so bad that I dreaded going to sleep. Then one day, I read 2 Corinthians 10:3-5. Dreams are from God, or they are ungodly thoughts that need to be dealt with. Once I saw that I could bring my dreams and thoughts captive, I acted upon this knowledge. I prayed and asked the Lord to give me the wisdom and strength to bring every thought, including my dreams, captive to obey Christ. Immediately all dreams stopped except for those which were messages from God for me or others.

> *2 Corinthians 10:3-5 (ESV) For though we walk in the flesh, we are not waging war according to the flesh. 4 For the weapons of our warfare are not of the flesh but have divine power to destroy strongholds. 5 We destroy arguments and every lofty opinion raised against the knowledge of God, and take every thought captive to obey Christ,*

Suppose you have dreams or nightmares that you know are not messages from God. Then act. Ask God's forgiveness for any open door you gave these imaginations. Then by the authority of the Son of God, our Lord Jesus Christ, take the thoughts, dreams, and nightmares captive under the blood of the Lamb.

8
Overcoming the Fear of EVIL

1. *We can be free from the fear of MAN.*
2. *We can be free from the fear of DEATH.*
3. *We can be free from the fear of the FUTURE.*
4. *We can be free from the fear of DANGER.*
5. *We can be free from the fear of IDOLS.*
6. *We can be free from the fear of DREAMS.*
7. *We can be free from the fear of EVIL.*

Wickedness has been on the earth since the fall of Adam and Eve. The wickedness and violence so filled the land that God destroyed the earth by way of the flood. He said that it would once again be as in the days of Noah in that wickedness and violence would fill the land. We will see in our lifetime a level of unrighteousness that our forefathers could not have imagined possible one hundred or even fifty years ago.

Just because evil will run rampant does not mean we need to walk in the torment of fear over it. Wicked and evil will do wicked and evil activities. As an author, I like to take tours through bookstores and see what people purchase to read. I have been astonished as the book section on witchcraft has grown over the last few years. I stand in that section, praying against those who intend to purchase these books. In the witchcraft genre, people can buy books instructing them to cast demonic spells and curses on parents, teachers, pastors, and anyone deemed enemies.

How do you cope with the impending evil flooding the airwaves, social media, and school system? We see evil and lawlessness being promoted in every facet of our lives. From music to sports to news, we hear and see the cloud of corruption spreading, affecting everything in its path. How does that affect us? Is there a safe place left where we can walk in peace and safety?

There will come a day when we may feel like our lives are in constant danger of murder and that walking the streets is unsafe. The answer is not sticking your head in the sand, ignoring the evil, and hoping it all will disappear soon. The answer is certainly not keeping your head down, hoping to go unnoticed. When fear of evil starts to grip us, we need to act.

God is our strength and protector.

Remember that God is our strength and our protector. In Psalms 23, King David knew what walking in the shadow of death was like. When he first entered King Saul's place as a young boy, he had the King trying to kill him. Samuel, the prophet, anointed young David with oil and declared he would be the next King of Israel. The next stage found David in the ministry of dodging King Saul's spears. Throughout David's life, enemies tried to take his life. His son revolted against him and wanted to kill him. David's life was filled with evil planned to destroy him. He greatly understood God's word, commanding him not to fear evil.

1 Samuel 18:11 (ESV) And Saul hurled the spear, for he thought, "I will pin David to the wall." But David evaded him twice.

Psalms 23:4 (ESV) Even though I walk through the valley of the shadow of death, I will fear no evil, for

*you are with me; your rod and your staff, they comfort
me.*

People love the darkness over the light.

Our Lord Jesus Christ is the light that came in
darkness, but the people loved their darkness more than
light. They love evil more than the righteousness of God.
Today, we live in lawless times. Everyone wants to do
whatever is right in their own eyes, causing an amoral
society.

> *Matthew 4:16 (ESV) the people dwelling in darkness
> have seen a great light, and for those dwelling in the
> region and shadow of death, on them a light has
> dawned."*

Obedience promises protection.

We are promised that if we obey the commands of
our heavenly Father, He will protect us from the disasters
coming upon the earth. We do not need to fear the evil of
our day.

> *Proverbs 1:33 (ESV) but whoever listens to me will
> dwell secure and will be at ease, without dread of
> disaster."*

Pray for God's wisdom.

Evil is snowballing among the people of the world. It
would seem like everyone has lost the ability to think and
act with any logic. The Father tells us in Proverbs 3:21-26
that we need to be people with Godly wisdom. If we walk

with God, we will rest at night without fear when evil surrounds us. We do need to fear the sudden terror that will come.

> *Proverbs 3:21-26 (ESV) My son, do not lose sight of these— keep sound wisdom and discretion, 22 and they will be life for your soul and adornment for your neck. 23 Then you will walk on your way securely, and your foot will not stumble. 24 If you lie down, you will not be afraid; when you lie down, your sleep will be sweet. 25 Do not be afraid of sudden terror or of the ruin of the wicked, when it comes, 26 for the LORD will be your confidence and will keep your foot from being caught.*

I'm sure you have heard the term "garbage in, garbage out." We certainly cannot watch the daily news channels looking for good news. On a typical day, we will have a "bucketload" of bad news sprinkled with ten seconds or so of a "feel-good" story. A constant input of bad news, just like bad company, causes corruption of morals. We cannot fill our minds with stinking thinking and expect to be a solution to the ills in our society.

If we want good news, we must turn to God's Word. God promises we shall not be moved no matter what evil we face.

> *1 Corinthians 15:33 (ESV) Do not be deceived: "Bad company ruins good morals."*

> *Psalms 112:6-8 (ESV) For the righteous will never be moved; he will be remembered forever. 7 He is not afraid of bad news; his heart is firm, trusting in the LORD. 8 His heart is steady; he will not be afraid, until he looks in triumph on his adversaries.*

When you hear, don't fear.

Luke 21 is one of the prophetic end-times chapters. In Luke 21:9, we do not find "If you hear," but "When you hear." All the things in Luke 21 are yet to happen, and we may soon find ourselves walking through Biblical end-times prophecy. We are commanded not to fear.

> *Luke 21:9 (ESV) And when you hear of wars and tumults, do not be terrified, for these things must first take place, but the end will not be at once."*

Don't fear. Who can separate us from the love of God?

Romans 8:35-39 are some of the best comforting Scriptures in the Bible. No matter how wicked and evil the world gets, it cannot separate us from the love of God. All the trials, tribulations, and persecutions listed in the verses will befall humanity. We can either fear these things and lose our quality of life, or we can rejoice that in all of these, we are still the beloved of the Father.

> *Romans 8:35-39 (ESV) Who shall separate us from the love of Christ? Shall tribulation, or distress, or persecution, or famine, or nakedness, or danger, or sword? 36 As it is written, "For your sake we are being killed all the day long; we are regarded as sheep to be slaughtered." 37 No, in all these things we are more than conquerors through him who loved us. 38 For I am sure that neither death nor life, nor angels nor rulers, nor things present nor things to come, nor powers, 39 nor height nor depth, nor*

anything else in all creation, will be able to separate us from the love of God in Christ Jesus our Lord.

9
Overcoming the Fear of WAR

1. *We can be free from the fear of MAN.*
2. *We can be free from the fear of DEATH.*
3. *We can be free from the fear of the FUTURE.*
4. *We can be free from the fear of DANGER.*
5. *We can be free from the fear of IDOLS.*
6. *We can be free from the fear of DREAMS.*
7. *We can be free from the fear of EVIL.*
8. *We can be free from the fear of WAR.*

There have been wars somewhere on the earth since the beginning of history. I don't want you to fear over this next statement. In these last days, it will get really crazy as we see more and more wars and rumors of wars!

Do you find yourself glued to the news, wondering if we will fight another war somewhere in the world? We hear the term "WWIII" thrown around so much it seems it is not a matter of "if it will happen" but "when will it happen." Of course, any student of the Scriptures knows there will be an "End Times World War" that will end the age as we know it.

Wars will continually happen until the end.

Are you worried or concerned that when you hear a nation threatening someone with nuclear war, this would be the last war of all wars? The Scriptures tell us this would be the beginning of the end times and for us not to fear.

Matthew 24:6 (ESV) And you will hear of wars and rumors of wars. See that you are not alarmed, for this must take place, but the end is not yet.

Man, in his wickedness and greed, will lose the one thing that has kept us acting human: *the value of life.* More and more, we see the value of human life in the eyes of people diminishing. Mankind is becoming desensitized concerning pain, suffering, and death.

King David was a man of war.

King David was a man after God's own heart. David was also a man of war. His life as the King of Israel found him moving from battle to battle as the enemies of God's people came against them. In Psalms 27:3, we see a song of David that he needed to renew often. The soldiers were camped around him, but his heart would not fear. In his early role as King, He found His safety in the size of his armies. However, he learned he did not need the might of his troops but the ability to find his confidence in the Lord.

Psalms 27:3 (ESV) Though an army encamp against me, my heart shall not fear; though war arise against me, yet I will be confident.

We are to trust in the power of the Holy Spirit.

The prophet Zechariah brought forth the Word of the Lord and proclaimed, "It was not by might, nor by power, but by my Spirit."

> *Zechariah 4:6 (ESV) Then he said to me, "This is the word of the LORD to Zerubbabel: Not by might, nor by power, but by my Spirit, says the LORD of hosts.*

We are to trust in the name of the Lord.

King David said in Psalms 20:7 that the nation of Israel would trust in the name of the Lord.

> *Psalms 20:7 (ESV) Some trust in chariots and some in horses, but we trust in the name of the LORD our God.*

Salvation belongs to the Lord.

We need to embrace and cry out the words that King David proclaimed. David knew that in war, our salvation and victory belong to our God. We have seen our fair share of wars in America, but nothing like those coming soon. Fear can paralyze us mentally and emotionally. In fear, we lose our ability to trust God for protection and welfare. When we walk in fear, we see wars as bad choices of politicians instead of God's plan for the end of the ages being played out.

> *Psalms 3:3-8 (ESV) But you, O LORD, are a shield about me, my glory, and the lifter of my head. 4 I cried aloud to the LORD, and he answered me from his holy hill. Selah 5 I lay down and slept; I woke again, for the LORD sustained me. 6 I will not be afraid of many thousands of people who have set themselves against me all around. 7 Arise, O LORD! Save me, O my God! For you strike all my enemies on the cheek; you break the teeth of the wicked. 8 Salvation belongs to the LORD; your blessing be on your people! Selah*

"Do not be afraid, for those who are with us are more than those who are with them."

When the world's armies rise in the last days against Israel and faithful Christians, we will see that the army of God, His angels, will fight with us and for us. Fear not!

> *2 Kings 6:15-17 (ESV) When the servant of the man of God rose early in the morning and went out, behold, an army with horses and chariots was all around the city. And the servant said, "Alas, my master! What shall we do?" 16 He said, "Do not be afraid, for those who are with us are more than those who are with them." 17 Then Elisha prayed and said, "O LORD, please open his eyes that he may see." So the LORD opened the eyes of the young man, and he saw, and behold, the mountain was full of horses and chariots of fire all around Elisha.*

10
Overcoming the Fear of
IMAGINATIONS (Fearful Thinking)

1. We can be free from the fear of MAN.
2. We can be free from the fear of DEATH.
3. We can be free from the fear of the FUTURE.
4. We can be free from the fear of DANGER.
5. We can be free from the fear of IDOLS.
6. We can be free from the fear of DREAMS.
7. We can be free from the fear of EVIL.
8. We can be free from the fear of WAR.
9. We can be free from the fear of IMAGINATIONS.

When addressing the topic of fearful thinking, I am reminded of times many years ago when I was staying in my house alone. I was robbed back in 1974. I woke up and saw the robber in the room. When I jumped up out of bed, he fled from the room and got away. I remember how unsettled I felt knowing that my space had been violated. I felt uneasy at night for a long time, even after salvation.

You know the feeling when you are home alone, and it is 02:00 am, and a noise awakens you. It sounded as though someone was trying to get into the door. Then every noise in the house becomes an enemy in the imagination. The sounds are like creaking and settling foundations, ice machines in the refrigerator dropping a new supply of ice, the wind blowing the tree limbs, and neighborhood cats and dogs.

Before long, the imaginations have run away into a place called fear, and the tormentor is at work. You know the feeling. It seems like your heart is setting in the middle of your throat, and your pulse is pounding so fast and hard you think your head will burst. Then the brain kicks in overdrive with random images and thoughts convincing you that sleep will certainly not come any time soon. Then you find yourself flopping in the bed like a fish freshly pulled from the stream. Yes. It is time to get out of bed to read a book or put on a boring movie you don't want to have to concentrate on.

How do you stop the emotional and mental train rolling down this wild track of fearful imaginations? The Scriptures say that because of how things will become, people will consistently think of fear, and their hearts will fail them. This means heart attacks will increase because of fear. If imaginations are false, like the sounds in the night, we are not to dwell on these things in our thinking. If imaginations are actual, like the crime rate, wars, and rumors of war, we should not dwell on these things in our thoughts.

I remember how my mother would let her thoughts or imaginations run away. In 1977, I was living in Las Vegas. I called my mom, who lived in a small community in Virginia, and told her that Debby and I were driving across the country to see everyone. I soon realized this phone call was a bad idea. Although long, Debby and I enjoyed our two-day trip from Las Vegas to Staunton, Virginia. However, Mom was a basket case. She almost became functionally incapacitated from extreme emotional distress and nervousness. In her mind, we had wrecked and were dead on the roadside somewhere along the route. Upon arriving safely at moms, she relayed her worries. I realized I could not tell her of any travel plans Debby, and I made.

Everything that can be shaken will be shaken.

Don't get me wrong. There are going to be natural disasters unparalleled in the history of mankind. The earth and the heavens will be destroyed in the end times. There are preppers getting themselves ready for such end times disasters as though they will be able to weather the end of the age foretold in Matthew 24. Some extreme preppers are readying themselves for impending catastrophic disasters. Many of these preppers find it challenging to enjoy life now because of their fear of the impending disasters of the future. All the worry you and I can muster up cannot change what will happen. We must choose to rejoice in the Lord today instead of fearing by allowing our imagination to run wide about what might come tomorrow.

> *Luke 21:25-26 (ESV) "And there will be signs in sun and moon and stars, and on the earth distress of nations in perplexity because of the roaring of the sea and the waves, 26 people fainting with fear and with foreboding of what is coming on the world. For the powers of the heavens will be shaken.*

> *Hebrews 12:26-29 (ESV) At that time his voice shook the earth, but now he has promised, "Yet once more I will shake not only the earth but also the heavens." 27 This phrase, "Yet once more," indicates the removal of things that are shaken—that is, things that have been made—in order that the things that cannot be shaken may remain. 28 Therefore let us be grateful for receiving a kingdom that cannot be shaken, and thus let us offer to God acceptable worship, with reverence and awe, 29 for our God is a consuming fire.*

Don't let your imagination invent trouble.

Instead of allowing our imaginations to invent trouble, pain, disaster, and death, the Apostle Paul gave us these words from the Holy Spirit. We are to renew our minds. In renewing our minds, God tells us what we should be thinking. Instead of fearing imagination, we should be thinking about things that are true, honorable, just, pure, lovely, commendable, excellent things and things that are worthy of praise.

> *Philippians 4:6-9 (ESV) do not be anxious about anything, but in everything by prayer and supplication with thanksgiving let your requests be made known to God. 7 And the peace of God, which surpasses all understanding, will guard your hearts and your minds in Christ Jesus. 8 Finally, brothers, whatever is true, whatever is honorable, whatever is just, whatever is pure, whatever is lovely, whatever is commendable, if there is any excellence, if there is anything worthy of praise, think about these things. 9 What you have learned and received and heard and seen in me— practice these things, and the God of peace will be with you.*

11
Overcoming the Fear of our ENEMIES

1. *We can be free from the fear of MAN.*
2. *We can be free from the fear of DEATH.*
3. *We can be free from the fear of the FUTURE.*
4. *We can be free from the fear of DANGER.*
5. *We can be free from the fear of IDOLS.*
6. *We can be free from the fear of DREAMS.*
7. *We can be free from the fear of EVIL.*
8. *We can be free from the fear of WAR.*
9. *We can be free from the fear of IMAGINATIONS.*
10. *We can be free from the fear of our ENEMIES.*

What is the most anyone can do to us? Paul says that if they bless him, then he wins. If his enemies beat him, then he wins. If his enemies kill him, then he wins. Paul sees the persecution of a believer as a win-win situation. If God cannot protect us from our enemies, then can He really save our souls?

> *Psalms 118:6 (ESV) The LORD is on my side; I will not fear. What can man do to me?*

When we think about the term "enemies," we typically think about someone who has wronged us somehow. However, the Scriptures give us a different concept of who our enemies are. The Scriptures tell us we have three principal enemies; the world (the worldly system, fallen nature, and lost people), Satan (all demons), and our flesh.

1. The World

The present world system includes fallen nature and all who are spiritually lost. We are commanded to love the lost but not to love the worldly system. The world is driven by the lust of the flesh, the lust of the eyes, and the pride of life.

> *1 John 2:15-17 (ESV) Do not love the world or the things in the world. If anyone loves the world, the love of the Father is not in him. 16 For all that is in the world—the desires of the flesh and the desires of the eyes and pride of life—is not from the Father but is from the world. 17 And the world is passing away along with its desires, but whoever does the will of God abides forever.*

2. Satan and the demonic

The devil and his demonic host are personal fallen angelic beings who attempt to drive Christians away from the faith and our Lord Jesus Christ. They are enemies we all face.

> *1 Peter 5:8-10 (ESV) Be sober-minded; be watchful. Your adversary the devil prowls around like a roaring lion, seeking someone to devour. 9 Resist him, firm in your faith, knowing that the same kinds of suffering are being experienced by your brotherhood throughout the world. 10 And after you have suffered a little while, the God of all grace, who has called you to his eternal glory in Christ, will himself restore, confirm, strengthen, and establish you.*

3. Our flesh

The flesh is our old sinful Adamic nature. It is the nature we inherit at birth. We were given a new character after our Lord Jesus Christ when we were saved. We were given an incorruptible seed. However, we still battle in the soulish realm with the lust of the flesh, the lust of the eyes, and the pride of life. We must put off the old man and put on the new man. We must choose to die to ourselves and allow Christ to live His life in and through us.

> *Galatians 2:20 (ESV) I have been crucified with Christ. It is no longer I who live, but Christ who lives in me. And the life I now live in the flesh I live by faith in the Son of God, who loved me and gave himself for me.*

> *Ephesians 4:22-24 (ESV) to put off your old self, which belongs to your former manner of life and is corrupt through deceitful desires, 23 and to be renewed in the spirit of your minds, 24 and to put on the new self, created after the likeness of God in true righteousness and holiness.*

God declares that those who are spiritually lost are enemies to God, the Lord Jesus Christ, the Holy Spirit, and believers. If they're enemies to the cross, they are enemies to us. We're to love them. However, we must realize they are enemies. We're not to fear them, but we are to pray for them and bless them. The Scripture says if we love the world, we are at enmity or strife against God. Jesus even said that some of our greatest enemies would be members of our household. Father will turn against son, and mother will turn against daughter.

Luke 12:51-53 (ESV) Do you think that I have come to give peace on earth? No, I tell you, but rather division. 52 For from now on in one house there will be five divided, three against two and two against three. 53 They will be divided, father against son and son against father, mother against daughter and daughter against mother, mother-in-law against her daughter-in-law and daughter-in-law against mother-in-law."

Matthew 10:34-37 (ESV) "Do not think that I have come to bring peace to the earth. I have not come to bring peace, but a sword. 35 For I have come to set a man against his father, and a daughter against her mother, and a daughter-in-law against her mother-in-law. 36 And a person's enemies will be those of his own household. 37 Whoever loves father or mother more than me is not worthy of me, and whoever loves son or daughter more than me is not worthy of me.

Luke 6:22-23 (ESV) "Blessed are you when people hate you and when they exclude you and revile you and spurn your name as evil, on account of the Son of Man! 23 Rejoice in that day, and leap for joy, for behold, your reward is great in heaven; for so their fathers did to the prophets.

What is our reaction to the schemes of our enemies?

Psalms 56:2-13 gives us a vivid word picture of the plans and activities of those who are our enemies. They will oppose us fiercely on all sides. We have a few choices in how we will react to this attack by those who oppose us.

We can fight back with an eye for an eye attitude. However, we will soon find ourselves overpowered and outnumbered. And it is not the way our Lord told us to respond.

We can use the fright and flight approach, also called the acute stress response. It is the reaction taken when someone feels the presence of something mentally or physically terrifying. Some will stay and fight, which we covered in the first response in fighting back. However, when we fear our enemies, we are more prone to run away to safety.

In the two responses to fear, which are the fight or flight responses, there are typically three stages.

The Alarm Stage

The first is the alarm stage. This alarm stage is the initial awareness of fear and danger. This stage is what prepares the body to either fight or flee.

The Resistance Stage

The second stage is the resistance stage. In the resistance stage, the body, mind, and emotions attempt to balance, normalize, and recover from the initial shock of fear. Those who walk in a lot of fear never seem to recover to a normal recovery point.

The Exhaustion Stage

The third stage is the exhaustion stage. The exhaustion stage is when the first two stages are repeated over short periods of little rest. It would be classified as chronic stress or fear. The lack of calm and rest causes the body to feel exhausted, breaks down the immune system, and causes damage and illnesses.

What can we do?

So, what are we to do when surrounded by enemies? The enemies could be people, demons, or even things like germs.

Praise.

The Scriptures tell us, as in Psalms 56:2-13 to place our trust in God. We must learn how to be praising people.

> *Psalms 56:2-13 (ESV) my enemies trample on me all day long, for many attack me proudly. 3 When I am afraid, I put my trust in you. 4 In God, whose word I praise, in God I trust; I shall not be afraid. What can flesh do to me? 5 All day long they injure my cause; all their thoughts are against me for evil. 6 They stir up strife, they lurk; they watch my steps, as they have waited for my life. 7 For their crime will they escape? In wrath cast down the peoples, O God! 8 You have kept count of my tossings; put my tears in your bottle. Are they not in your book? 9 Then my enemies will turn back in the day when I call. This I know, that God is for me. 10 In God, whose word I praise, in the LORD, whose word I praise, 11 in God I trust; I shall not be afraid. What can man do to me? 12 I must perform my vows to you, O God; I will render thank offerings to you. 13 For you have delivered my soul from death, yes, my feet from falling, that I may walk before God in the light of life.*

Renew the mind.

One of my favorite verses in God's Word is Romans 8:31. Who can stand against us? Think about this. Who can stand against us if God is for us? Let this renew your mind and then bring your fear under the control of God's Word.

Romans 8:31 (ESV) What then shall we say to these things? If God is for us, who can be against us?

I have to laugh when I read about things the Apostle Paul went through and how he reacted to them. He made many different lists of things he faced just to stand faithful for our Lord Jesus Christ. 2 Corinthians 4:7-11 is one such list. He called our bodies "jars of clay." That is funny when I see this word picture in my mind. But then he talks about the glorious treasure we have in these jars of clay. Let's look at how Paul suffered for Christ without fear.

1. *Afflicted in every way, but not crushed.*
2. *Perplexed but not driven to despair.*
3. *Persecuted, but not forsaken.*
4. *Struck down but not destroyed.*

2 Corinthians 4:7-11 (ESV) But we have this treasure in jars of clay, to show that the surpassing power belongs to God and not to us. 8 We are afflicted in every way, but not crushed; perplexed, but not driven to despair; 9 persecuted, but not forsaken; struck down, but not destroyed; 10 always carrying in the body the death of Jesus, so that the life of Jesus may also be manifested in our bodies. 11 For we who live are always being given over to death for Jesus' sake, so that the life of Jesus also may be manifested in our mortal flesh.

We will face death at the hands of our enemies.

In Philippians 1:20-24 Paul reveals that he knew he was about to face death at the hands of his enemies. He spoke about his impending death in different Scriptures. Each is a lesson for us on being proactive in our daily walk. Our enemies are growing daily as contempt and hatred for genuine Christians increase. Instead of fearing his enemies and death, Paul embraced his ministry in life and death. He desired to live and die so that Christ would be honored. He preferred to stay alive only if it meant he could exalt Christ among the people. However, his heart desired to be absent from the body in order to be present in glory with Christ. We overcome the fear of our enemies by overcoming the fear of death, which we covered in chapter three.

> *Philippians 1:20-24 (ESV) as it is my eager expectation and hope that I will not be at all ashamed, but that with full courage now as always Christ will be honored in my body, whether by life or by death. 21 For to me to live is Christ, and to die is gain. 22 If I am to live in the flesh, that means fruitful labor for me. Yet which I shall choose I cannot tell. 23 I am hard pressed between the two. My desire is to depart and be with Christ, for that is far better. 24 But to remain in the flesh is more necessary on your account.*

12
Overcoming the Fear of PUNISHMENT

1. We can be free from the fear of MAN.
2. We can be free from the fear of DEATH.
3. We can be free from the fear of the FUTURE.
4. We can be free from the fear of DANGER.
5. We can be free from the fear of IDOLS.
6. We can be free from the fear of DREAMS.
7. We can be free from the fear of EVIL.
8. We can be free from the fear of WAR.
9. We can be free from the fear of IMAGINATIONS.
10. We can be free from the fear of our ENEMIES.
11. We can be free from the fear of PUNISHMENT.

I remember growing up in the mountains in Virginia, where children were to be seen but not heard. My siblings and I were a little rambunctious and seemed to get in trouble by fighting each other. Mama would say wait until your Daddy gets home. Right away came the fear of punishment because we knew when Daddy came home, we would get spanked. And true to form, when Daddy got home, we all had our turn bending over the couch and receiving our punishment.

I brought some of this fear of punishment into adulthood and my Christian life. I wanted to obey God and man out of honor and respect, but most of the time, it was out of fear. Maybe you were punished for something justly or unjustly, and it has left you fearing retribution for actions or statements made.

Most of us hate confrontation. I have been called on the carpet a few times in different employment situations where I made a decision that was less than favorable for my supervisors. Being a pastor for over forty years, I have had many disagreeable moments with unhappy church members. I have found that people believe everything you preach and teach as long as you preach and teach what they already believe. This pastoral calling has given me ample opportunities to develop the fear of punishment. The average tenure of pastors is less than three years. Therefore, many pastors struggle with the fear of being fired. This termination is especially intense when there are small school-age children involved. No one wants to uproot their family in the middle of a school year to relocate to another city or state as the dad starts a new pastoral position.

Reading God's word and learning God's character taught me to overcome the fear of punishment of either man or God.

The chastening of the Lord.

One of my most comforting Scriptures is Hebrews 12:5-12. When I tell people this is a comforting Scripture, they look at me a little odd because it speaks about the chastisement of God on His children. There is joy in knowing that when God chastises us, it reveals evidence or proof that we are His children. Those who God does not chasten are not His children. Another comfort in this Scripture is that God never spanks us out of anger or in an unrighteous way. He always disciplines us in love and for our good, hoping it will lead us to righteousness. Hebrews 12:11 tells us that the discipline of God seems painful at the moment but yields the fruit of righteousness. Proverbs 3:11-

12 and Job 5:17 carries the same teaching as Hebrews chapter 12 concerning the discipline of the Lord.

> *Hebrews 12:5-12 (ESV) And have you forgotten the exhortation that addresses you as sons? "My son, do not regard lightly the discipline of the Lord, nor be weary when reproved by him. 6 For the Lord disciplines the one he loves, and chastises every son whom he receives." 7 It is for discipline that you have to endure. God is treating you as sons. For what son is there whom his father does not discipline? 8 If you are left without discipline, in which all have participated, then you are illegitimate children and not sons. 9 Besides this, we have had earthly fathers who disciplined us and we respected them. Shall we not much more be subject to the Father of spirits and live? 10 For they disciplined us for a short time as it seemed best to them, but he disciplines us for our good, that we may share his holiness. 11 For the moment all discipline seems painful rather than pleasant, but later it yields the peaceful fruit of righteousness to those who have been trained by it. 12 Therefore lift your drooping hands and strengthen your weak knees,*

> *Proverbs 3:11-12 (ESV) My son, do not despise the LORD's discipline or be weary of his reproof, 12 for the LORD reproves him whom he loves, as a father the son in whom he delights.*

> *Job 5:17 (ESV) "Behold, blessed is the one whom God reproves; therefore despise not the discipline of the Almighty.*

Avoid discipline through self-evaluation.

The Apostle Paul tells us in 1 Corinthians 11:31-32 that we should judge ourselves. The word "judge" in this passage does not mean casting a sentence but evaluating ourselves. We do not evaluate ourselves based on what's right in our own eyes but according to the Word of God and the righteousness of God. If we evaluate ourselves according to the righteousness of God, we know that God will discipline anything in us that doesn't look like His character, and in doing so, we will not face the end-times judgment.

> *1 Corinthians 11:31-32 (ESV) But if we judged ourselves truly, we would not be judged. 32 But when we are judged by the Lord, we are disciplined so that we may not be condemned along with the world.*

We may face persecution (punishment) for righteousness' sake.

If anyone could understand unjust punishment or being persecuted for righteousness sake, it would be the Apostle Paul. He explains in 2 Corinthians 6:3-10 that some of the hardships he faced came as a result of preaching the gospel message. On one hand, he would say the punishment was sorrowful at the moment, but on the other hand, he rejoiced in trials, tribulations, persecutions, and unjust punishment. Preaching the gospel left him poor, yet he was rich in God. In man's eyes, he would be seen as a man with nothing, yet he possessed everything.

Missing God's punishment

We covered the fear of man in Chapter 2. If we do not fear man, we should not fear man's punishment, even if it's unjust and unto death (see Chapter 3). The Scriptures tell us if they hated Christ, how much more will they hate us, and if they persecuted Him, how much more will we be persecuted? We should bless and praise God when persecuted for righteousness' sake. The one punishment we do not want to fall under is the punishment of God. How do we avoid or bypass the punishment of God? We waive God's punishment by putting our faith in the Father, our Lord Jesus Christ, God's Word, and standing faithful to the end.

> *2 Corinthians 6:3-10 (ESV) We put no obstacle in anyone's way, so that no fault may be found with our ministry, 4 but as servants of God we commend ourselves in every way: by great endurance, in afflictions, hardships, calamities, 5 beatings, imprisonments, riots, labors, sleepless nights, hunger; 6 by purity, knowledge, patience, kindness, the Holy Spirit, genuine love; 7 by truthful speech, and the power of God; with the weapons of righteousness for the right hand and for the left; 8 through honor and dishonor, through slander and praise. We are treated as impostors, and yet are true; 9 as unknown, and yet well known; as dying, and behold, we live; as punished, and yet not killed; 10 as sorrowful, yet always rejoicing; as poor, yet making many rich; as having nothing, yet possessing everything.*

13
Overcoming the Fear of DARKNESS

1. We can be free from the fear of MAN.
2. We can be free from the fear of DEATH.
3. We can be free from the fear of the FUTURE.
4. We can be free from the fear of DANGER.
5. We can be free from the fear of IDOLS.
6. We can be free from the fear of DREAMS.
7. We can be free from the fear of EVIL.
8. We can be free from the fear of WAR.
9. We can be free from the fear of IMAGINATIONS.
10. We can be free from the fear of our ENEMIES.
11. We can be free from the fear of PUNISHMENT.
12. We can be free from the fear of DARKNESS.

The darkness that can cause us to fear is not limited to the darkness of the night. It could also be the darkness of a situation, such as persecution, distress, or emotional, mental, and physical attacks. It could be spiritual darkness in our lives due to sins not confessed and spiritually dealt with. It could be a lack of God's Word with us. Whatever our darkness is, we can rest in the assurance of God and His Word of protection and oversight. We can confess the spiritual, mental, or emotional darkness and enter His light.

Have you ever faced spiritual, mental, or emotional darkness? In 1992, I underwent spiritual and emotional darkness as intense as a thousand midnights. I thought I would die. This dark season was the first and last time I passionately argued with God about what was happening. I felt a deep fear in this darkness because I didn't know where it came from or how to escape it. It lasted three weeks, and the Father taught me lessons I may not have learned otherwise. I was delivered from the darkness and learned a valuable lesson on what Biblical praise was and what it was not.

God's protection in the dark places

Song of Solomon is a beautiful love story between King Solomon and the Shulamite woman. It is also an allegory describing the love relationship between God and His people, known as "the church." Song of Solomon 3:7 speaks of sixty valiant men. These were mighty men of war to protect the King's maiden as she went through the dangerous wilderness to the wedding.

> *Song of Solomon 3:7-8 (ESV) Behold, it is the litter of Solomon! Around it are sixty mighty men, some of the mighty men of Israel, 8 all of them wearing swords and expert in war, each with his sword at his thigh, against terror by night.*

When traveling through a wilderness, a royal procession was always in danger of attack. Bedouins were always prepared to attack a caravan, especially a marriage procession. The robbers hoped they might obtain jewels. If they captured the bride, they hoped for a heavy ransom for her redemption by the Bridegroom and her friends. In this case, the maiden need not worry or fear the darkness because she is being protected by her beloved.

This passage answers people's fears about God's church on this earth. This text shows us we do not need to fear the darkness because God, our Father, and Jesus, our Bridegroom, guard His church. His angels, God's valiant guards, are watching over His children. The Father's messengers who protect His church are well-armed, well-trained, always ready, and watchful.

Ten thousand will fall by our side.

Psalms 91:1-7 is a mighty promise of being under the Father's protection. Therefore, we have no reason to fear the darkness. Ten thousand may fall around us, but we who trust in the Lord will be saved and protected.

> *Psalms 91:1-7 (ESV) He who dwells in the shelter of the Most High will abide in the shadow of the Almighty. 2 I will say to the LORD, "My refuge and my fortress, my God, in whom I trust." 3 For he will deliver you from the snare of the fowler and from the deadly pestilence. 4 He will cover you with his pinions, and under his wings you will find refuge; his faithfulness is a shield and buckler. 5 You will not fear the terror of the night, nor the arrow that flies by day, 6 nor the pestilence that stalks in darkness, nor the destruction that wastes at noonday. 7 A thousand may fall at your side, ten thousand at your right hand, but it will not come near you.*

Instead of fear, we can sleep in the darkness as David did.

We should not fear the darkness or the thousands that stand against us. We read in Psalms 3:4-6 that King David knew there were armies against him to take his life and throne. However, he lay down peacefully and could sleep because he knew the Lord sustained him.

> *Psalms 3:4-6 (ESV) I cried aloud to the LORD, and he answered me from his holy hill. Selah 5 I lay down*

*and slept; I woke again, for the LORD sustained me.
6 I will not be afraid of many thousands of people who
have set themselves against me all around.*

The wicked should fear the darkness.

We find in 1 Samuel 2:9-10 that the wicked have reason to fear the darkness, for they will be cut off. However, those who remain faithful will be guarded.

*1 Samuel 2:9-10 (ESV) "He will guard the feet of his
faithful ones, but the wicked shall be cut off in
darkness, for not by might shall a man prevail. 10 The
adversaries of the LORD shall be broken to pieces;
against them he will thunder in heaven. The LORD
will judge the ends of the earth; he will give strength
to his king and exalt the horn of his anointed."*

If we trust, the Father will light our path in the dark times.

Our God is a lamp that lightens the paths of darkness. His Word is a lamp to our feet and a light in our path.

*2 Samuel 22:29-37 (ESV) For you are my lamp, O
LORD, and my God lightens my darkness.*

*Psalms 119:105 (ESV) Nun Your word is a lamp to
my feet and a light to my path.*

14
Overcoming the Fear of SPIRITS

1. We can be free from the fear of MAN.
2. We can be free from the fear of DEATH.
3. We can be free from the fear of the FUTURE.
4. We can be free from the fear of DANGER.
5. We can be free from the fear of IDOLS.
6. We can be free from the fear of DREAMS.
7. We can be free from the fear of EVIL.
8. We can be free from the fear of WAR.
9. We can be free from the fear of IMAGINATIONS.
10. We can be free from the fear of our ENEMIES.
11. We can be free from the fear of PUNISHMENT.
12. We can be free from the fear of DARKNESS.
13. We can be free from the fear of SPIRITS.

The spirit world can be a little unsettling to most believers. When it comes to spirits, sometimes we take the "out of sight, out of mind" approach. Think about it. You have read the Scriptures concerning Jesus casting out demons. You have also read all the Scriptures that tell us to go out in the world and preach the good news. We usually give a big "yes and Amen" to the command to go into the highways and byways with the gospel message. However, those same Scriptures tell us to cast out demons.

Matthew 10:7-8 (ESV) And proclaim as you go, saying, 'The kingdom of heaven is at hand.' 8 Heal the sick, raise the dead, cleanse lepers, cast out demons. You received without paying; give without pay.

Mark 16:17-18 (ESV) And these signs will accompany those who believe: in my name they will cast out demons; they will speak in new tongues; 18 they will pick up serpents with their hands; and if they drink any deadly poison, it will not hurt them; they will lay their hands on the sick, and they will recover."

Matthew 7:22-23 (ESV) On that day many will say to me, 'Lord, Lord, did we not prophesy in your name, and cast out demons in your name, and do many mighty works in your name?' 23 And then will I declare to them, 'I never knew you; depart from me, you workers of lawlessness.'

Matthew 10:1 (ESV) And he called to him his twelve disciples and gave them authority over unclean spirits, to cast them out, and to heal every disease and every affliction.

Luke 9:1-2 (ESV) And he called the twelve together and gave them power and authority over all demons and to cure diseases, 2 and he sent them out to proclaim the kingdom of God and to heal.

Luke 9:49-50 (ESV) John answered, "Master, we saw someone casting out demons in your name, and we tried to stop him, because he does not follow with us." 50 But Jesus said to him, "Do not stop him, for the one who is not against you is for you."

Mark 6:12-13 (ESV) So they went out and proclaimed that people should repent. 13 And they cast out many demons and anointed with oil many who were sick and healed them.

Acts 8:5-7 (ESV) Philip went down to the city of Samaria and proclaimed to them the Christ. 6 And the crowds with one accord paid attention to what was being said by Philip, when they heard him and saw the signs that he did. 7 For unclean spirits, crying out with a loud voice, came out of many who had them, and many who were paralyzed or lame were healed.

Think about it for a moment. When, if ever, have you commanded a demon to come out of a person? If never, why not? There are demonized people around us almost daily. Are we afraid of demonic spirits and the unknown spiritual realm? Let's face it, very few Christians share their faith by preaching the good news because of fear. If we fear sharing the gospel message that Jesus loves us and will save us, we certainly will have a fear of commanding the demonic out of someone. These statements are not meant to condemn us but to provoke us to overcome the fears that paralyze us from doing the Word of God.

This fear of spirits can cover a wide range of the spirit world. First, we see that it refers to our Lord Jesus Christ as He walked on water. When the disciples saw Jesus, they thought He was a spirit or ghost. It can also refer in the Old Testament to the manifestations of God, like the burning bush. It can also refer to the manifestation of angels walking among us, as seen in the Old and New Testaments. The angels can speak to us and reveal themselves physically. It can also refer to demonic spirits that can speak or reveal themselves physically. No matter the situation, we are not to walk in a tormented state of fear.

What we witness today is a fascination with ghosts and zombies. This common fascination with ghosts is certainly not limited to our generation. In Matthew 14:26-27

71

the disciples saw Jesus walking on water, and immediately their first thought was that they saw a ghost.

> *Matthew 14:26-27 (ESV) But when the disciples saw him walking on the sea, they were terrified, and said, "It is a ghost!" and they cried out in fear. 27 But immediately Jesus spoke to them, saying, "Take heart; it is I. Do not be afraid."*

Mary's first encounter with the angel startled her. Luke 1:29 says she was greatly troubled. Well, that is an understatement. Her fear was so physically evident that in Luke 1:30, we read that the angel told her not to be afraid.

> *Luke 1:28-30 (ESV) And he came to her and said, "Greetings, O favored one, the Lord is with you!" 29 But she was greatly troubled at the saying, and tried to discern what sort of greeting this might be. 30 And the angel said to her, "Do not be afraid, Mary, for you have found favor with God.*

In the burning bush example recorded in Exodus 3:4-6, we see that the "spirit" is the Lord speaking to Moses through a burning bush that is not consumed. Spontaneous combustion of dried tumbleweeds in the desert is not unusual. It was not that the bush was burning that caught Moses' attention. The fact that the bush burned without being consumed attracted Moses' attention.

> *Exodus 3:2 (ESV) And the angel of the LORD appeared to him in a flame of fire out of the midst of a bush. He looked, and behold, the bush was burning, yet it was not consumed.*

When Moses came closer to look at this strange event, the angel of the Lord spoke to him. The phrase "the angel of the Lord" in the Old Testament frequently refers to the pre-incarnate Lord Jesus Christ.

> *Exodus 3:4-6 (ESV) When the LORD saw that he turned aside to see, God called to him out of the bush, "Moses, Moses!" And he said, "Here I am." 5 Then he said, "Do not come near; take your sandals off your feet, for the place on which you are standing is holy ground." 6 And he said, "I am the God of your father, the God of Abraham, the God of Isaac, and the God of Jacob." And Moses hid his face, for he was afraid to look at God.*

In other examples, we find that the fear of spirits included demons. The key to remember is that the demons fear Jesus. They also fear the Holy Spirit within us.

> *Matthew 8:28-32 (ESV) And when he came to the other side, to the country of the Gadarenes, two demon-possessed men met him, coming out of the tombs, so fierce that no one could pass that way. 29 And behold, they cried out, "What have you to do with us, O Son of God? Have you come here to torment us before the time?" 30 Now a herd of many pigs was feeding at some distance from them. 31 And the demons begged him, saying, "If you cast us out, send us away into the herd of pigs." 32 And he said to them, "Go." So they came out and went into the pigs, and behold, the whole herd rushed down the steep bank into the sea and drowned in the waters.*

We have the authority to cast demons out and away just as our Lord Jesus Christ did. I will list many Scriptures.

Faith comes by hearing and hearing by the Word. Read these Scriptures out loud and listen to what the Father is saying to us concerning our authority over the demonic.

> *Mark 1:23-27 (ESV) And immediately there was in their synagogue a man with an unclean spirit. And he cried out, 24 "What have you to do with us, Jesus of Nazareth? Have you come to destroy us? I know who you are—the Holy One of God." 25 But Jesus rebuked him, saying, "Be silent, and come out of him!" 26 And the unclean spirit, convulsing him and crying out with a loud voice, came out of him. 27 And they were all amazed, so that they questioned among themselves, saying, "What is this? A new teaching with authority! He commands even the unclean spirits, and they obey him."*

> *Mark 5:2-13 (ESV) And when Jesus had stepped out of the boat, immediately there met him out of the tombs a man with an unclean spirit. 3 He lived among the tombs. And no one could bind him anymore, not even with a chain, 4 for he had often been bound with shackles and chains, but he wrenched the chains apart, and he broke the shackles in pieces. No one had the strength to subdue him. 5 Night and day among the tombs and on the mountains he was always crying out and cutting himself with stones. 6 And when he saw Jesus from afar, he ran and fell down before him. 7 And crying out with a loud voice, he said, "What have you to do with me, Jesus, Son of the Most High God? I adjure you by God, do not torment me." 8 For he was saying to him, "Come out of the man, you unclean spirit!" 9 And Jesus asked him, "What is your name?" He replied, "My name is Legion, for we are many." 10 And he begged him earnestly not to send them out of the country. 11 Now*

a great herd of pigs was feeding there on the hillside, 12 and they begged him, saying, "Send us to the pigs; let us enter them." 13 So he gave them permission. And the unclean spirits came out and entered the pigs; and the herd, numbering about two thousand, rushed down the steep bank into the sea and drowned in the sea.

Luke 4:31-36 (ESV) And he went down to Capernaum, a city of Galilee. And he was teaching them on the Sabbath, 32 and they were astonished at his teaching, for his word possessed authority. 33 And in the synagogue there was a man who had the spirit of an unclean demon, and he cried out with a loud voice, 34 "Ha! What have you to do with us, Jesus of Nazareth? Have you come to destroy us? I know who you are—the Holy One of God." 35 But Jesus rebuked him, saying, "Be silent and come out of him!" And when the demon had thrown him down in their midst, he came out of him, having done him no harm. 36 And they were all amazed and said to one another, "What is this word? For with authority and power he commands the unclean spirits, and they come out!"

Mark 3:11-12 (ESV) And whenever the unclean spirits saw him, they fell down before him and cried out, "You are the Son of God." 12 And he strictly ordered them not to make him known.

James 4:7 (ESV) Submit yourselves therefore to God. Resist the devil, and he will flee from you.

1 Peter 5:8-9 (ESV) Be sober-minded; be watchful. Your adversary the devil prowls around like a roaring lion, seeking someone to devour. 9 Resist him, firm in your faith, knowing that the same kinds of suffering are being experienced by your brotherhood throughout the world.

If we walk in fear of spirits, we may miss an angelic visitation delivering a message from the throne room of heaven. We may miss being ministered to by a guardian angel the Lord sent to serve us when we need care or protection. We may miss the opportunity of ministering to a fellow human being, seeing them set free by casting out a tormenting spirit. We may miss the chance of shutting down and silencing demonic activity that may be happening in our church service, which, if left unchecked, could cause relational division or a church split. We may miss the opportunity to pray over someone's home and break demonic strongholds that have tormented the family in nightmares and fears. Lest you think I might be speaking of abstract situations, I can testify that the Father has used me in every example listed above.

15
Overcoming the SPIRIT OF FEAR

1. We can be free from the fear of MAN.
2. We can be free from the fear of DEATH.
3. We can be free from the fear of the FUTURE.
4. We can be free from the fear of DANGER.
5. We can be free from the fear of IDOLS.
6. We can be free from the fear of DREAMS.
7. We can be free from the fear of EVIL.
8. We can be free from the fear of WAR.
9. We can be free from the fear of IMAGINATIONS.
10. We can be free from the fear of our ENEMIES.
11. We can be free from the fear of PUNISHMENT.
12. We can be free from the fear of DARKNESS.
13. We can be free from the fear of SPIRITS.
14. We can be free from the SPIRIT OF FEAR.

I saved the "spirit of fear" for last because I want everyone to remember that this is a demonic spirit that tries to keep us walking in fear, fright, worry, and anxiety and away from the maturity of the love of God. Some folks seem to fear everything. They worry about everything and always see the negative happening to people. Some people won't eat certain foods because they have a high choking risk. Some won't fly because, in their minds, fear makes airplane crashes far more common than car wrecks.

Do you battle with fear in general? Do you feel anxious and seem to be overly consumed with worry?

First, I must say this. Worry is a sin. Being fearful is a sin. I know that we are aware of this, but somehow, we think that God understands, and we justify ourselves out of the sinfulness of worry and fear. Until we think about these things, the way the Father feels about them, and the way the Word teaches about them, we will never be free.

> *Matthew 6:25 (ESV) "Therefore I tell you, do not be anxious about your life, what you will eat or what you will drink, nor about your body, what you will put on. Is not life more than food, and the body more than clothing?*

> *Matthew 6:31-34 (ESV) Therefore do not be anxious, saying, 'What shall we eat?' or 'What shall we drink?' or 'What shall we wear?' 32 For the Gentiles seek after all these things, and your heavenly Father knows that you need them all. 33 But seek first the kingdom of God and his righteousness, and all these things will be added to you. 34 "Therefore do not be anxious about tomorrow, for tomorrow will be anxious for itself. Sufficient for the day is its own trouble.*

Look at the three things that are ours if we choose not to give in to the spirit of fear. We can walk in God's power, God's love, God's peace, and God's sound mind. Since this is the last fear, let's break 2 Timothy 1:6-7 down word by word.

> *2 Timothy 1:6-7 (ESV) For this reason I remind you to fan into flame the gift of God, which is in you through the laying on of my hands, 7 for God gave us a spirit not of fear but of power and love and self-control.*

The Greek word in 2 Timothy 1:7 for spirit is "pneuma," which is a current of air or a breath or breeze blast. It can refer to the spirit of a man (the innermost man). The word spirit can refer to a demonic spirit. Or the word spirit can refer to the Person of the Holy Spirit. The context in which it is used will tell us which use of spirit is correct.

The Greek word for fear is "deilia, " meaning timidity or fear.

The Greek word for power here is "dunamis" and means force, power, ability, might, and violence.

The Greek word for love here is "agape," which means affection, a love feast, or dear love. It is the word we have for God's unconditional love.

The Greek word for sound mind is "sophronismos," meaning self-control and discipline.

Don't these three things, God's power, love, and a sound mind, look much better than walking in the spirit of fear? Then why don't believers choose to walk in them instead of fear?

At some time, we all will battle with the familiar. The familiar is what we have done or felt physically, emotionally, and mentally for so long that it is the comfortable and convenient choice. We don't have to think about it because it is our typical mode of operation.

Since we know the familiar well, we tend to drift back to it no matter what training we have received. It takes us hearing something at least seven times before we really HEAR it. It takes hearing and doing something at least twenty-one times before it starts changing our habits and way of life. So, if you read this book one time, you will know that your fear is wrong, but you have not heard it enough to get the truth deep in your soul to make a change. Read and reread this and the Scriptures given until you have achieved a change to walk without fear.

If this were easy, everyone would do it. Most of us operate like water. Water seeks its own level and takes the path of least resistance. Water seeking its own level is like saying we will do what is right in our own eyes. This mentality was what the Father had against many of the Kings and Judges in the Old Testament. Taking the path of least resistance is doing what is the easiest, which is returning to the familiar. Many call it "Microwave Christianity." We want instant success and maturity without paying the price of growing up in the Lord.

We know how to walk in fear and rest in our own strength. It takes a continual exercise of seeking the heart of the Father to break out of the familiar and actually walk in the trust and love of the Father.

16
The Good Kind Of Fear: Loving And Fearing God

The love of God and the fear of God go hand in hand. Read Psalms 104 because there are at least thirty reasons to fear God in those Scriptures. The fear of the Lord is having a Godly honor, respect, and holy reverence for the King of Glory. Great blessings are listed in the Word of God to those who fear the Lord. I will give the points of blessings and a Scripture and leave the commentary to your personal study.

Fearing God Is The Beginning Of Knowledge And Wisdom

Proverbs 1:7 (ESV) The fear of the LORD is the beginning of knowledge; fools despise wisdom and instruction.

Proverbs 9:10 (ESV) The fear of the LORD is the beginning of wisdom, and the knowledge of the Holy One is insight.

Fearing God Determines Destiny

Proverbs 1:29-33 (ESV) Because they hated knowledge and did not choose the fear of the LORD, 30 would have none of my counsel and despised all my reproof, 31 therefore they shall eat the fruit of their way, and have their fill of their own devices. 32 For the simple are killed by their turning away, and the complacency of fools destroys them; 33 but whoever listens to me will dwell secure and will be at ease, without dread of disaster."

Fearing God Helps In Departing From Evil Habits

Proverbs 3:5-9 (ESV) Trust in the LORD with all your heart, and do not lean on your own understanding. 6 In all your ways acknowledge him, and he will make straight your paths. 7 Be not wise in your own eyes; fear the LORD, and turn away from evil. 8 It will be healing to your flesh and refreshment to your bones. 9 Honor the LORD with your wealth and with the firstfruits of all your produce;

Proverbs 16:6-9 (ESV) By steadfast love and faithfulness iniquity is atoned for, and by the fear of the LORD one turns away from evil. 7 When a man's ways please the LORD, he makes even his enemies to be at peace with him. 8 Better is a little with righteousness than great revenues with injustice. 9 The heart of man plans his way, but the LORD establishes his steps.

Fearing God Helps To Have A Proper Biblical Hate For Evil

Proverbs 8:13 (ESV) The fear of the LORD is hatred of evil. Pride and arrogance and the way of evil and perverted speech I hate.

Fearing God Prolongs Our Days On The Earth

Proverbs 10:27 (ESV) The fear of the LORD prolongs life, but the years of the wicked will be short.

Fearing God Gives Strong Confidence

> *Proverbs 14:26 (ESV) In the fear of the LORD one has strong confidence, and his children will have a refuge.*

Fearing God Is A Fountain Of Life To Our Soul

> *Proverbs 14:27 (ESV) The fear of the LORD is a fountain of life, that one may turn away from the snares of death.*

Fearing God Produces Satisfaction

> *Proverbs 15:15-16 (ESV) All the days of the afflicted are evil, but the cheerful of heart has a continual feast. 16 Better is a little with the fear of the LORD than great treasure and trouble with it.*

Fearing God Instructs In Wisdom

> *Proverbs 15:32-33 (ESV) Whoever ignores instruction despises himself, but he who listens to reproof gains intelligence. 33 The fear of the LORD is instruction in wisdom, and humility comes before honor.*

Fearing God Tends To Life

> *Proverbs 19:22-23 (ESV) What is desired in a man is steadfast love, and a poor man is better than a liar. 23 The fear of the LORD leads to life, and whoever has it rests satisfied; he will not be visited by harm.*

Fearing God Gives Riches, Honor, And Life

Proverbs 22:3-4 (ESV) The prudent sees danger and hides himself, but the simple go on and suffer for it. 4 The reward for humility and fear of the LORD is riches and honor and life.

Fearing God Brings Blessings

Ecclesiastes 8:12-13 (ESV) Though a sinner does evil a hundred times and prolongs his life, yet I know that it will be well with those who fear God, because they fear before him. 13 But it will not be well with the wicked, neither will he prolong his days like a shadow, because he does not fear before God.

17
Prayer is the key to overcoming FEAR

W e should see prayer as God's invitation for us to visit with Him. What is your primary reason for praying? I know that may seem like a dumb question, but we do need to evaluate why we pray. Some people only pray what I call "911" crisis praying. Of course, we know from Psalms 50:15 God will hear us in our time of trouble and deliver us.

Psalms 50:15 (ESV) and call upon me in the day of trouble; I will deliver you, and you shall glorify me."

But that is not the only praying we're called to do. If you want to evaluate your prayer life, write down what you prayed for after you finish praying. Were most of your prayers consumed with physical, relational, or financial needs and desires? I chose these three because, as a pastor for over 45 years, most of the prayer requests I have received were combined in these three categories. People needed physical healing, relational healing, a job, or someone in their job was giving them a hard time.

Even though we have significant needs in our daily life, prayer should be more than a conscious effort to seek God for a need. Prayer is a call of God's love to come and fellowship. God's call to prayer proves our ability to stand before His presence. Prayer proves we are made righteous in Christ with the ability and right to stand before Him without guilt or condemnation. We are invited and will be welcomed to the throne room. Entering the Father's presence should be done with God's Word on our lips and faith in our hearts. It is holding God's Word up to Him like a mirror as we agree with Him in prayer. There cannot be a genuine demand upon the Father or Son without them knowing and experiencing our request through the prayer of faith. When our need touches the Lord, it makes a demand upon His ability to meet that need.

> *Matthew 11:28 (ESV) Come to me, all who labor and are heavy laden, and I will give you rest.*

> *Hebrews 4:16 (ESV) Let us then with confidence draw near to the throne of grace, that we may receive mercy and find grace to help in time of need.*

Will we walk in fear at times? Yes! We will even face times when we feel as though we will die or be killed. Realizing that God sees us and protects us will keep us from fear or staying in fear. Remember, we are responsible for our emotions. We choose to become angry, and we choose to fear. We can use God's Word and the knowledge of His presence and decide not to be angry or fearful. Read again what King David wrote in the 23rd Psalm.

> *Psalms 23:4 (ESV) Even though I walk through the valley of the shadow of death, I will fear no evil, for you are with me; your rod and your staff, they comfort me.*

David asks us an important question in Psalms 27:1. God is our strength, so who will we fear?

Psalms 27:1 (ESV) Of David. The LORD is my light and my salvation; whom shall I fear? The LORD is the stronghold of my life; of whom shall I be afraid?

When we have an opportunity to fear, we should not look at how big and dangerous our situation is. We should not look at how outnumbered we are. We must remember how big our God is; He is our strength and refuge. The whole army of Israel looked at the giant Goliath and said, "He is too big to fight or kill." David, the young shepherd boy, looked at the giant and basically declared, "He is too big to miss." Let's look at the story. We see in 1 Samuel 17:4 that Goliath was around 9 ½ feet tall.

1 Samuel 17:4 (ESV) And there came out from the camp of the Philistines a champion named Goliath of Gath, whose height was six cubits and a span.

In 1 Samuel 17:8-11, we see that Goliath challenged the best soldier in Israel's army to come out and fight against him. However, King Saul and his army shuttered in fear.

1 Samuel 17:8-11 (ESV) He stood and shouted to the ranks of Israel, "Why have you come out to draw up for battle? Am I not a Philistine, and are you not servants of Saul? Choose a man for yourselves, and let him come down to me. 9 If he is able to fight with me and kill me, then we will be your servants. But if I prevail against him and kill him, then you shall be our servants and serve us." 10 And the Philistine said, "I defy the ranks of Israel this day. Give me a man, that we may fight together." 11 When Saul and all Israel heard these words of the Philistine, they were dismayed and greatly afraid.

We see in 1 Samuel 17:22-24 that Goliath had made the same challenge for thirty days. David, the young shepherd boy, visited his brothers at Israel's camp and heard the defying threats from the Philistine giant. David witnessed the fear of the army of Israel firsthand.

> *1 Samuel 17:22-24 (ESV) And David left the things in charge of the keeper of the baggage and ran to the ranks and went and greeted his brothers. 23 As he talked with them, behold, the champion, the Philistine of Gath, Goliath by name, came up out of the ranks of the Philistines and spoke the same words as before. And David heard him. 24 All the men of Israel, when they saw the man, fled from him and were much afraid.*

David asked in 1 Samuel 17:26 what would be done for the man who killed the giant. David wanted to know firsthand what reward the champion would receive.

> *1 Samuel 17:26 (ESV) And David said to the men who stood by him, "What shall be done for the man who kills this Philistine and takes away the reproach from Israel? For who is this uncircumcised Philistine, that he should defy the armies of the living God?"*

In 1 Samuel 17:32-36 the young shepherd boy, David, told King Saul he would fight Goliath. Saul was amused at the zeal of the young man. However, David revealed a Biblical principle we need to hear. Many within the church always want to go to another country to teach and preach. I knew a group who always wanted to go to another country, stick their fists up in the heavens, and do spiritual warfare against the principalities in a region.

However, David had the correct pattern and testimony. The Biblical principle is "Be faithful in a little, and God will give you more." "Be faithful in another man's field, and God will give you your field." The key is to have a testimony of faithfulness.

David told the King the story of the lion and the bear. When the lions and bears attacked his sheep, David would strike them down and deliver the sheep. David said he would treat the Philistine giant as he did the lions and bears.

> *1 Samuel 17:32-36 (ESV) And David said to Saul, "Let no man's heart fail because of him. Your servant will go and fight with this Philistine." 33 And Saul said to David, "You are not able to go against this Philistine to fight with him, for you are but a youth, and he has been a man of war from his youth." 34 But David said to Saul, "Your servant used to keep sheep for his father. And when there came a lion, or a bear, and took a lamb from the flock, 35 I went after him and struck him and delivered it out of his mouth. And if he arose against me, I caught him by his beard and struck him and killed him. 36 Your servant has struck down both lions and bears, and this uncircumcised Philistine shall be like one of them, for he has defied the armies of the living God."*

David had a heart after God and knew the victory would be the Lord's. Read what he said in 1 Samuel 17:37.

> *1 Samuel 17:37 (ESV) And David said, "The LORD who delivered me from the paw of the lion and from the paw of the bear will deliver me from the hand of this Philistine." And Saul said to David, "Go, and the LORD be with you!"*

David testified about the One True God of Israel in 1 Samuel 17:43-46. He knew his strength was in the Lord, and his weapon was the name that was above every name. He did not fear because he understood what trusting God meant.

> *1 Samuel 17:43-46 (ESV) And the Philistine said to David, "Am I a dog, that you come to me with sticks?" And the Philistine cursed David by his gods. 44 The Philistine said to David, "Come to me, and I will give your flesh to the birds of the air and to the beasts of the field." 45 Then David said to the Philistine, "You come to me with a sword and with a spear and with a javelin, but I come to you in the name of the LORD of hosts, the God of the armies of Israel, whom you have defied. 46 This day the LORD will deliver you into my hand, and I will strike you down and cut off your head. And I will give the dead bodies of the host of the Philistines this day to the birds of the air and to the wild beasts of the earth, that all the earth may know that there is a God in Israel, 47 and that all this assembly may know that the LORD saves not with sword and spear. For the battle is the LORD's, and he will give you into our hand."*

In 1 Samuel 17:49-50, we found that David did not pick up a new weapon to fight Goliath. He used the weapon he was familiar with. He had five stones in his bag but only took one out. Why? He trusted in God, and he trusted in his faithfulness to the hard work it took to be skilled in the slingshot. The one thing we find consistent in the early life of David is his faithfulness in the small things. We live in a microwave instant society where everyone wants what they want quickly without any inconvenience. This attitude has permeated the church causing immature believers to seek the easiest solution to a problem or a life of compromise.

1 Samuel 17:49-50 (ESV) And David put his hand in his bag and took out a stone and slung it and struck the Philistine on his forehead. The stone sank into his forehead, and he fell on his face to the ground. 50 So David prevailed over the Philistine with a sling and with a stone, and struck the Philistine and killed him. There was no sword in the hand of David.

David showed that when we stand fearless, trusting in God, the enemy that was once boasting of victory flees in fear.

1 Samuel 17:51 (ESV) Then David ran and stood over the Philistine and took his sword and drew it out of its sheath and killed him and cut off his head with it. When the Philistines saw that their champion was dead, they fled.

James 4:7 (ESV) Submit yourselves therefore to God. Resist the devil, and he will flee from you.

Psalms 27:3 (ESV) Though an army encamp against me, my heart shall not fear; though war arise against me, yet I will be confident.

Psalms 46:1 reminds us that God is our strength, refuge, and help.

Psalms 46:1 (ESV) To the choirmaster. Of the Sons of Korah. According to Alamoth. A Song. God is our refuge and strength, a very present help in trouble.

God cannot lie. We have His promise that if we pray, listen, and obey Him, we shall dwell in safety and be free from fear. We will lie down and sleep in peace.

Numbers 23:19 (ESV) God is not man, that he should lie, or a son of man, that he should change his mind. Has he said, and will he not do it? Or has he spoken, and will he not fulfill it?

Proverbs 1:32-33 (ESV) For the simple are killed by their turning away, and the complacency of fools destroys them; 33 but whoever listens to me will dwell secure and will be at ease, without dread of disaster."

Proverbs 3:23-26 (ESV) Then you will walk on your way securely, and your foot will not stumble. 24 If you lie down, you will not be afraid; when you lie down, your sleep will be sweet. 25 Do not be afraid of sudden terror or of the ruin of the wicked, when it comes, 26 for the LORD will be your confidence and will keep your foot from being caught.

FEAR NOT!
    Trust and obey,
    For there's no other way,
        To be happy in JESUS.

Grace and Peace.

More Books By Charles Morris

Look for eBooks (EB), paperbacks (PB), & hardcovers (HC)

1. **THE FOUR POSITIONS OF THE HOLY SPIRIT**: *Beside Us, Within Us, Upon Us, and Filling Us (EB, PB, HC) (2014 02 17; 2021 10 02, 1st, 2nd, & 3rd Editions).*
2. **BORN AGAIN**: *Having a Personal Relationship with God (EB, PB, HC) (2021 07 09, 1st & 2nd Editions).*
3. **THE 10 CHARACTERISTICS OF A SPIRIT-FILLED CHURCH**: *The Spirit-Filled Life Bible Study (EB, PB, 1st Edition).*
4. **THE COVENANT OF SALT**: *Everyone Will be Salted with Fire (EB, PB, HC) (2021 10 03, 1st Edition).*
5. **THE PARABLE OF THE FOUR SOILS**: *The Key to the Mystery of the Kingdom of God. (EB, PB, HC) (2021 06 23, 1st Edition).*
6. **THE FIVE EVIDENCES OF SALVATION**: *How Do I Know That I'm Saved? (EB, PB, HC) (2021 09 10, 1st & 2nd Editions).*
7. **FAITHFUL**: *How Can I Be Faithful to God? (EB, PB, HC) (2021 06 20, 1st & 2nd Editions).*
8. **HOSEA**: *What Does the Book of Hosea Teach Us? (EB, PB, HC) (2021 05 28, 1st Edition).*
9. **PREPARING OURSELVES TO HEAR THE VOICE OF GOD**: *Do You Want to Hear the Voice of God? Book 1 (EB, PB, HC) (2021 06 09, 1st & 2nd Editions).*
10. **FIFTEEN WAYS TO HEAR THE VOICE OF GOD**: *Do You Want to Hear the Voice of God? Book 2. (EB, PB, HC) (2021 06 11, 1st & 2nd Editions).*

A Careless Heart; The Son, A Rebellious Heart. *(EB, PB, 1st Edition)*.

27. **THE MYSTERY OF LAWLESSNESS UNLEASED.** *(EB, PB, HC, 1st Edition)*.
28. **THE CHRONOLOGICAL BOOK OF END TIMES:** *11 Undeniable Prophecies Of The End Times. (EB, PB, HC) (2022 03 16, 1st Edition)*.
29. **IS ATHEISM DEAD?:** *The Unbelieving Unbelievers Epidemic. Book 1 of the "They Walk Among Us" series. (EB, PB, HC) (2022 03 01, 1st Edition)*.
30. **WHEREVER YOU GO TRAVEL JOURNAL:** *The Ultimate Guide To All 50 States. (PB, 1st Edition)*.
31. **WHEREVER YOU GO TRAVEL JOURNAL (FOR TEENS):** *The Ultimate Guide To All 50 States. (PB, 1st Edition)*.
32. **THE TOPICAL JOURNAL:** *Journal Like A Veteran (PB 1st Edition)*.
33. **THE TOPICAL JOURNAL:** *Don't Just Sit There, JOURNAL. For women. (PB, 1st Edition)*.
34. **THE TOPICAL JOURNAL:** *Journaling That Impacts Your Life. (PB, 1st Edition). PB 1st Edition*.
35. **WHEREVER YOU GO, TRAVEL JOURNAL (FOR THE GUYS):** *The Ultimate Guide to All 50 States. (PB, 1st Edition)*.
36. **THE TOPICAL JOURNAL:** *Don't Just Sit There, Journal. For Men. (PB, 1st Edition)*.
37. **IS RELIGION DEAD?:** *The Believing Unbelievers Epidemic. Book 2 of the "They Walk Among Us" series. (EB, PB, HC) (2022 06 18, 1st Edition)*.
38. **UNLEASHED:** *Understanding The Mystery Of Lawlessness. (EB, PB, HC) (2022 06 26, 1st Edition)*.
39. **I FEEL LIKE I'M LOSING MY FAITH:** *How Do I Fix My Faulty Faith? (EB, PB, 1st Edition)*.
40. **WE NEED FAITH:** *Faith After Doubt. (EB, PB, HC) (2022 07 25, 1st Edition)*.
41. **THE HOLY BIBLE THE KING JAMES VERSION OF**

THE OLD AND NEW TESTAMENTS -ANNOTATED-*: (EB 2022 08 06)*

42. *IS CHRISTIAN IMMATURITY DEAD?: The Unbelieving Believers Epidemic. Book 3 of the "They Walk Among Us" series. (EB, PB, HC) (2022 09 02, 1st Edition).*

43. ***THE PARABLE OF THE WHEAT AND TARES****: A Guide To Understanding The Kingdom Of God. (EB, PB, HC) (2022 10 08, 1ST Edition)*

44. ***GO TELL IT ON THE MOUNTAIN:*** *The Great Commission; God's Plan To Reach The World. (EB, PB, HC) (2022 11 17 1st Edition)*

45. ***THE COST OF DISCIPLESHIP:*** *Making Disciples In Turbulent Times; 2 Timothy 2:2 Discipling 101. (EB, PB, HC) (2022 11 23 1st Edition)*

46. ***THE POWER OF ONE MORE:*** *Mastering The Art Of Leadership. (EB, PB, HC) (2022 12 02 1st Edition)*

47. ***THE GOSPEL ACCORDING TO LUKE:*** *Luke 15: The Road To Restoration And Fellowship. (EB, PB, HC) (2022 12 19 1st Edition)*

48. ***THE GOSPEL ACCORDING TO JESUS:*** *Reflections On The Last Teaching Of Jesus: Commentary On John 16. (EB, PB, HC) (2023 01 14 1st Edition)*

49. ***I AM*** *More Than Enough In Christ. 180-Day "I AM" Journal. (EB, PB, HC) (Light Blue, Dark Blue, Gold, Peach, Light Pink, Dark Pink) (2023 01 17)*

50. ***SIX ENEMIES OF FAITH:*** *Quick Read Bible Study That Will Challenge Your Stinking Thinking. (EB) (2023 01 18)*

About The Author

CHARLES is passionate about the manifested presence of God, seeing the Father's authentic Biblical leadership taking their position of grace and authority, and working towards seeing true Biblical unity in the Spirit and unity of the faith within the body of Christ. He served the Lord and others in the pastorate for more than 40 years, leading almost 8,000 people to a personal knowledge of the Lord Jesus Christ.

In 2000, Charles founded Raising the Standard International Ministry (RSIM), assisting pastors, spiritual leaders, and the body of Christ in pursuing these key objectives.

In 2018, Charles founded Raising the Standard International Publishing (RSIP) to self-publish his books and assist other believers in pursuing their dream of getting the passion of their hearts printed. Charles has written and published more than 35 books.

Charles is an evangelist and church planter known for his uncompromising approach to God's Word without denominational or religious bias. He has the unique ability to use word pictures to paint the truth of God's Word. His uncompromising message instills the virtues of honor and respect for other believers, whether they are in a position of authority, being a peer, or have been entrusted to his shepherding and care. Charles' key message for believers is to die daily to self, embrace the beauty in personal brokenness, and walk in faith and the power of the Holy Spirit.

Charles Morris

NOTES

Made in the USA
Columbia, SC
20 July 2023

20611352R00059